Editor-in-Chief and Founder:
   Lyndon H. LaRouche, Jr.
Editorial Board: *Lyndon H. LaRouche, Jr. , Helga
   Zepp-LaRouche, Robert Ingraham, Tony
   Papert, Gerald Rose, Dennis Small, Jeffrey
   Steinberg, William Wertz*
Co-Editors: *Robert Ingraham, Tony Papert*
Managing Editor: *Nancy Spannaus*
Technology: *Marsha Freeman*
Books: *Katherine Notley*
Ebooks: *Richard Burden*
Graphics: *Alan Yue*
Photos: *Stuart Lewis*
Circulation Manager: *Stanley Ezrol*

INTELLIGENCE DIRECTORS
Counterintelligence: *Jeffrey Steinberg, Michele
   Steinberg*
Economics: *John Hoefle, Marcia Merry Baker,
   Paul Gallagher*
History: *Anton Chaitkin*
Ibero-America: *Dennis Small*
Russia and Eastern Europe: *Rachel Douglas*
United States: *Debra Freeman*

INTERNATIONAL BUREAUS
Bogotá: *Miriam Redondo*
Berlin: *Rainer Apel*
Copenhagen: *Tom Gillesberg*
Houston: *Harley Schlanger*
Lima: *Sara Madueño*
Melbourne: *Robert Barwick*
Mexico City: *Gerardo Castilleja Chávez*
New Delhi: *Ramtanu Maitra*
Paris: *Christine Bierre*
Stockholm: *Ulf Sandmark*
United Nations, N.Y.C.: *Leni Rubinstein*
Washington, D.C.: *William Jones*
Wiesbaden: *Göran Haglund*

ON THE WEB
e-mail: eirns@larouchepub.com
www.larouchepub.com
www.executiveintelligencereview.com
www.larouchepub.com/eiw
Webmaster: *John Sigerson*
Assistant Webmaster: *George Hollis*
Editor, Arabic-language edition: *Hussein Askary*

EIR (ISSN 0273-6314) *is published weekly
(50 issues), by EIR News Service, Inc.,
P.O. Box 17390, Washington, D.C. 20041-0390.
(703) 297-8434*

European Headquarters: E.I.R. GmbH, Postfach
Bahnstrasse 9a, D-65205, Wiesbaden, Germany
Tel: 49-611-73650
Homepage: http://www.eir.de
e-mail: info@eir.de
Director: Georg Neudecker

Montreal, Canada: 514-461-1557
eir@eircanada.ca

Denmark: EIR - Danmark, Sankt Knuds Vej 11,
basement left, DK-1903 Frederiksberg, Denmark.
Tel.: +45 35 43 60 40, Fax: +45 35 43 87 57. e-mail:
eirdk@hotmail.com.

Mexico City: EIR, Sor Juana Inés de la Cruz 242-2
Col. Agricultura C.P. 11360
Delegación M. Hidalgo, México D.F.
Tel. (5525) 5318-2301
eirmexico@gmail.com

Crush the British Coup Against the President

Your Congressman Just Voted For War with Russia

July 31—On July 25, in a flagrantly unconstitutional action, the United States House of Representatives voted 419 to 3 to impose harsh sanctions against the nation of Russia. This action was followed two days later when the United States Senate voted 98 to 2 for the sanctions bill. This legislation imposes new sanctions, codifies existing penalties into law—including the harsh sanctions imposed by Barack Obama in 2016—and gives Congress veto power over any attempt by President Trump to remove or relax them. With these votes, the Congress has acted to effect an illegal seizure of the direction of foreign policy from the duly elected President. The primary argument that was utilized in justifying these anti-Russia measures was the lie that Russia interfered in the 2016 U.S. election, through "hacking" and other means.

The combined vote, in both houses, was 517 to 5. Such folly and lemming-like uniform cowardice has probably not been seen in the United States Congress since the passage of the Gulf of Tonkin Resolution in 1964, a resolution which passed the Congress by a vote of 504 to 2. That vote, from fifty-three years ago, ushered in a decade of war, which killed tens of thousands of Americans and millions of Vietnamese, and plunged the United States into a deep cultural and political despair. Today, the stakes for the United States—and for all of humanity—are much, much higher. The U.S. Congress, backed by the establishment media, has now acted to wreck the peace initiatives of the Trump administration and put the world back on a trajectory toward war.

There were five heroes who opposed this madness. They are: Senators Rand Paul (R-KY) and Bernie Sand-ers (I-VT), and Representatives Justin Amash (R-MI), John Duncan (R-TN) and Thomas Massie (R-KY). Not a single Democrat voted against the sanctions bill!

This vote for a policy of war is the result of the decades-long penetration of the United States government by allies and servants of the British Empire. Recall that it was Tony Blair and his fake *Dodgy Dossier* which set the stage for the 2003 invasion of Iraq. Recall that it was Britain which partnered with the Bush and Obama administrations in effecting a massive NATO military expansion, in the overthrow and murder of Libya's Muammar Gaddafi in 2011, in the 2014 Nazi coup d'etat in the Ukraine, and in continuing military confrontation with China in East Asia. It is the British System, and its legacy of geopolitics, which is behind all of this, and it is their corruption of U.S. intelligence agencies, the establishment news media and the leadership of both major political parties which has brought us to this moment of crisis.

Under Barack Obama, the United States, in alliance with Britain, implemented a policy of aggressive military confrontation with both Russia and China—this, accompanied by a parallel policy of illegal global "regime changes," as well as support for ISIS terrorists. Donald Trump, in his election campaign, vowed to reverse these policies, and as President, he has taken steps to correct the worst of these crimes. These steps include, but are not limited to, his personal discussions with both Xi Jinping and Vladimir Putin, as well as his decision to end the CIA's covert program to arm and train Syrian rebels now battling the government of Bashar al-Assad.

The insane and cowardly U.S. Congress has now

voted to sabotage these peace initiatives by the President and to revive the war drive of the Obama administration, a war drive fully endorsed by Hillary Clinton. This is not what the people of the United States voted for in 2016. Forty-three percent of Democratic Party voters cast their ballots for Bernie Sanders, stating emphatically their desire to overturn the neocon policies of the Obama regime. In the general election, Donald Trump won thirty states and defeated Hillary Clinton by almost eighty electoral votes. Congress has now acted, not only against the peace initiatives of President Trump, but in flagrant defiance of the wishes of the American people.

At the same time, this action occurs as Lyndon LaRouche and other economists are warning of a near-term eruption of a financial and banking crisis worse than 2007-2008. Such a monetary blow-out will unleash chaos in the United States and Europe, the repercussions of which can only heighten the strategic danger. The stakes for humanity have never been this high.

Lies, Lies, and More Lies

During the past week, three interventions have been made which utterly demolish all claims that the Russian government "hacked" DNC computers in an effort to influence the 2016 U.S. elections. The evidence presented in these interventions utterly demolishes the rationale put forward to justify the new anti-Russia sanctions.

On July 24, the Veterans Intelligence Professionals for Sanity (an organization comprised of former FBI, NSA, CIA and other intelligence experts) released a Memorandum for President Trump, wherein they demonstrate that the release of DNC files far more likely came from a "leak," not a "hack," and they also document, conclusively, that the allegations of Russian involvement are a fairy tale, a created narrative which has no evidence to support it. On July 27, Scott Ritter, a former United Nations weapons inspector in Iraq, published his own review of the VIPS findings, titled "Time to Reassess the Roles Played by Guccifer 2.0 and Russia in the DNC 'Hack.'" Although Ritter takes exception to a few of the details contained in the Memorandum, he emphatically states, "To date there has been no examination worthy of the name regarding the facts that underpin the accusations at the center of the American argument against Russia—that the GRU hacked the DNC server and used Guccifer 2.0 as a conduit for the release of stolen documents in a manner designed to influence the American presidential election. The VIPS memorandum of July 24, 2017, questions the veracity of these claims. I believe these doubts are well founded." Then, on July 28, LaRouchePAC conducted a live interview with Ray McGovern, a former CIA analyst and former Chair of the National Intelligence Estimates, who was one of the signers of the VIPS Memorandum. In that interview, McGovern details the VIPS findings, including the computer forensic investigation of independent analyst Skip Folden, a retired IBM Program Manager for Information Technology. McGovern presents both the fraudulent nature of the Guccifer 2.0/Russian hacking narrative as well as the political motivations behind the lies. Further details of the evidence in this case will not be presented here. It is all available in the Internet links cited above.

It is important to recall that all of the current furor was kicked off with an announcement by Julian Assange on June 12, 2016, when he stated in a mass-circulation interview on Britain's ITV, that "we have emails related to Hillary Clinton which are awaiting publication." It is also important to emphasize that Assange has stated repeatedly that the documents he released came from a "leak," not a "hack." The documents posted by Assange proved conclusively that the DNC was covertly working with Hillary Clinton's campaign to run dirty tricks against then Presidential candidate Bernie Sanders. No one in the DNC or the Clinton entourage has ever denied the validity of the documents released by Assange; and the proof of DNC intervention into the primary process on behalf of Hillary Clinton, and against Bernie Sanders, was so strong that DNC Chairman Debbie Wasserman Schultz was forced to resign. The subsequent, alleged Guccifer 2.0 "hacks" were all designed to both discredit Assange and to create the false flag allegations of "Russian interference." It is precisely the fraudulent nature of the Guccifer 2.0 narrative that the VIPS Memorandum addresses.

The Coup d'Etat Means War

Lyndon LaRouche has stated that if the coup d'etat against President Trump succeeds, we will have nuclear war.

With certainty, it can be stated that both Russia and China are paying very close attention to developments in the United States. And they are taking steps to protect themselves. In Russia, on July 30, a Main Naval Parade was held for the first time in modern Russia's history—

on Navy Day, in celebration of the creation of the Russian Navy by Peter the Great in 1696. For the first time it brought together ships from Russia's Baltic, Black Sea, Northern, and Pacific Fleets, with its Caspian Flotilla, for a total of 5,000 sailors—and for the *first time in modern Russian history*, it was inspected by Russia's President. Putin's short address began by affirming that "Russia's history is inseparable from the victories of its courageous and fearless Navy. Our country's status as a strong marine power has been achieved through the brave acts of sailors and officers, the inventive talent of our shipbuilders and the daring exploits of sea explorers."

At the same time, in China, the 90th anniversary of the People's Liberation Army was celebrated by a military parade, *for the first time since the founding of the People's Republic of China in 1949*. It was held at Zhurihe, in the Inner Mongolia Autonomous Region, at China's biggest military base, which specializes in training in advanced technology. The *Wall Street Journal* reports that new, more-capable ICBMs were displayed with other new weapons, and 12,000 mechanized troops.

China's official news agency *Xinhua* reports that this was the first time President Xi Jinping has overseen such a large parade at a military base. It noted that "Late leaders Mao Zedong and Deng Xiaoping also inspected troops in the field at key moments in history."

In his address, Xi said, "The world is not all at peace, and peace must be safeguarded."

At this point, the members of Congress who voted for the sanctions bill against Russia can only be described as—witting or unwitting — accomplices in this war drive. And those members of Congress who continue to retail the line that the "Russians hacked the election," or that the "Trump is in bed with the Russians," stand exposed as imbeciles, liars, or cowards. There is no fourth choice. The political establishment—including leading elements of both major parties—wishes to overturn the election and to return the country to a policy of financial looting and a build-up for war.

It is clear that many members of Congress are terrified of the FBI, the CIA, and other parts of the Intelligence establishment, including such unofficial bodies as AIPAC. What many fail to see, is that behind these spook *apparatchiks*, lies the guiding hand of British geopolitics. We are dealing with a corrupted American political establishment. Last November, the American people did not vote for a policy of NATO expansion, nuclear weapons modernization, violent regime changes, military confrontation with China in Asia, and strategic confrontation with Russia.

The American people did not vote for war. Why did your Congressman?

Crises Shake the German Economy, U.S. Sanctions Must Be Rejected!

by Helga Zepp-LaRouche, chairwoman of the German political party, Civil Rights Movement Solidarity (BüSo)

July 29—Everything is happening at the same time: The emissions scandal in the German auto industry,[1] the revelations of a decades-long cartel agreement in the same industry, a geopolitical economic war by the U.S. Congress against Germany and Russia, a threatened trade war between the United States and the European Union (EU), EU threats against the German government, the predictable realization that the shift away from nuclear energy is a disaster, and the growing signs that we are on the verge of a new crash, worse than that of 2008. Are these all distinct, separate processes and phenomena, or is there an inner connection among them? And more importantly, is there a solution which will not force the proverbial "little people" to bear the burden—the consequences of these policies?

EDITORIAL

What we are currently experiencing are various symptoms of the collapse of the neoliberal trans-Atlantic system, of that economic and social model which replaced the vilified "minor virtues"—such as hard work, honesty, conscientiousness, trustworthiness, and courtesy—with the values of the shareholder and the IPOs, and of maximum profit, and in which the consensus of the elite is that the only crime is to get caught. Just as the taxpayers and depositors have had to pay for years now for the consequences of this shift in values due to the banking crisis, now it is the auto workers and their jobs, and the motorists, who are supposed to pay for the damage.

The situation is exacerbated by the fact that many of the players think they can seize the opportunity to make a name for themselves. One example is Environment Minister Barbara Hendricks who, during her latest visit to the Volkswagen plant at Wolfsburg, blamed the entire auto industry for all manner of cheating and consumer fraud, up to and including criminal behavior.

In fact, the industry's manipulations could lead to in-depth criminal prosecution. And it really doesn't speak well for the intelligence of the auto industry's boards of directors and managers that they thought they could carry out such a wide-ranging swindle—which of course required a large number of confidants—in secret for long. It has now been revealed that Audi technicians pointed to the fraudulent Volkswagen emissions manipulations in the United States as early as 2013 in an internal document, and strongly warned of possible punishments and payments for damages. Audi is a member of the Volkswagen Group.

But the root of the problem lies in the fact that the auto industry, as well as the entire German industrial elite, has given in to the various ecologically motivated policy guidelines, even though those industry leaders who have a clue about the natural sciences, know very well that behind the hypotheses of the connection between CO_2 and climate change, lie very different interests and intentions than those arguments which are brought forward. Not the least of these interests is profit for the banks and hedge funds, which make a killing with solar installations, wind parks, and the CO_2 emissions trade. Instead of fighting for scientific clarity on the climate controversy, they tolerate the suppression and ostracism of those scientists who question the calculations of the models that have constructed scenarios

---

1. Volkswagen programmed turbocharged direct injection diesel engines to activate some emissions controls only during laboratory emissions testing. The vehicles met U.S. standards for emission of mononitrogen oxides during regulatory testing, but otherwise emitted as much as 40 times more. Some eleven million cars worldwide had been programmed in this way when the U.S. Environmental Protection Agency discovered the fraud in September 2015.

of the connection between anthropogenic CO_2 and climate change.

The cowardice involved in capitulating to the dogma of anthropogenic climate change, almost inevitably led to the fact that the manipulation of auto emissions data posed no great ethical problem for them. The shift to a shareholder value society also unfortunately means that the boards of directors and the managers of the major companies lack scientific and technical competence, but have studied law. Volkswagen, by the way, had already created a sensation in 1987 with a foreign currency scandal.

Federal Transportation Minister Alexander Dobrindt, of the CSU, obviously wanted to seize the current opportunity as well, since, in the midst of the diesel scandal, he took the extraordinary measure of withdrawing certification of Porsche's Cayenne model. Porsche is also a member of the Volkswagen Group. And he imposed a compulsory recall of the 22,000 vehicles which had already been delivered throughout Europe, the cost of which must be borne entirely by the manufacturers—this action could entail a loss of jobs. The engines were produced by Audi, which was already charged with fraud by the head of Porsche's Works Council, which represents Porsche's workers.

Another aspect of these skyrocketing crises is, according to media reports in late July, an ongoing investigation by the EU Commission into a possible, decades-long illegal arrangement between the five German automakers—Daimler, BMW, Audi, Porsche, Volkswagen—and automotive supplier Bosch and possibly other companies, which set up 60 taskforces to coordinate vehicle development, suppliers, and markets. That is a practice which, by the way, is commonplace in other countries. German industry considers this investigation to be an EU attack.

The Attack by the U.S. Congress

As if these scandals were not enough to ruin the image of the industrial elite of the auto sector and other sectors of German industry (after that of the banks), and therefore weaken the economy overall, now there are the new sanctions against Russia adopted by both houses of the U.S. Congress. These sanctions are the height of madness, and are an attack on all of European industry and whatever sovereignty the European nations have left.

The sanctions bill is based on a whole array of fabricated charges and made-up stories, according to which Russian President Putin allegedly manipulated the 2016 election in the United States, and intends to influence all elections in other countries in the same way, including those of U.S. allies. Furthermore, the power of the U.S. President to change American foreign policy is made subject to congressional approval. That would include, for example, his ability to lift the sanctions that Obama imposed by decree.

This is a blatant attempt by Wall Street, the secret intelligence apparatus called the "deep state," and the mainstream media, to fence in the President—that is, to rob him of his constitutional power to determine policy. President Trump's approval of this bill signifies a highly dangerous escalation, in response to which President Putin has already announced countermeasures. This also means that any company that does not abide by these regulations is itself the target of sanctions, which—in total violation of international law—signifies the extraterritorial application of American law.

In Article 257, under the headline "Ukrainian energy security," the bill states, among other things, that it is U.S. policy "to continue to oppose the Nord Stream 2 pipeline"—from Russia to the European Union, through the Baltic Sea—"given its detrimental impacts on the

Gazprom

A Nord Stream pipeline facility.

European Union's energy security, gas market development in Central and Eastern Europe, and energy reforms in Ukraine"; and that "the United States Government should prioritize the export of United States energy resources in order to create American jobs, help United States allies and partners, and strengthen United States foreign policy."

The arrogant imperial domination couldn't be more crass: Germany and the other European countries are supposed to renounce the security of their own energy requirements, which in light of the situation in the Near and Middle East, and the inadequate remaining deposits in the North Sea, can only come from Russia—and instead import liquefied natural gas from the totally over-indebted fracking operations in the United States—for which import Europe is absolutely not technically prepared. Thus it's clear the real goal is to save the Wall Street banks, which are on the edge of implosion.

During his state visit to Finland, President Putin reacted promptly: This is an obvious, geopolitical attempt to impose the U.S.'s own advantage at the expense of its allies. These allies' reaction will show to what degree they still enjoy sovereignty. The first reactions, such as those from Austrian Chancellor Christian Kern and Michael Harms of the Eastern Committee of German Industry, charged that the sanctions imposed by the U.S. Congress were totally unacceptable.

'Russia-Gate' Debunked as a Fraud

The most important intervention against this ongoing coup against President Trump—which has seen the mainstream media, Wall Street, and the intelligence service holdovers from the Obama Administration succeed in creating an anti-Russian hysteria that dwarfs the worst excesses of the McCarthy period—came from the group of former intelligence experts called the Veteran Intelligence Professionals for Sanity (VIPS). They have provided the expert forensic evidence that Russia did not "hack" the Democratic Party computers during the 2016 election campaign, but that insiders downloaded the data onto a storage device. Thus Trump's argument has been totally confirmed: Russian hackers did not try to manipulate the U.S.

election, but those who are trying to annul the voters' electoral choice with "leaks" of real news and "fake news" are the problem.

The analysis now provided by the VIPS is of the utmost strategic significance, because it proves that there is no basis for "Russia-gate," that is, there is no basis for the assertion that Russia manipulated the American election. As VIPS member Ray McGovern pointed out in an interview with LaRouche PAC elsewhere in this issue of *EIR*, the line that Russia hacked the Democratic Party computers was given out by the party leadership in order to divert attention from the fact that the Hillary Clinton emails which Julian Assange of Wikileaks had published, proved that the party leadership had crushed Bernie Sanders' chances of being elected. It is urgently necessary that members of the VIPS be invited to testify as expert witnesses at investigations not only by the U.S. Congress, but also by the Bundestag. Because part of "Russia-gate" is also the assertion contained in the U.S. Congress' sanctions bill that Russia intends to influence elections all over the world, among them the upcoming Bundestag election in Germany.

The assertion of the supposed Russian influence in the election was kept up by the transatlantic Establishment after Trump's election. The artificially created hysteria was supposed to discourage the President from carrying out his election promise of putting the U.S. relationship with Russia—which Obama had totally ruined—on a sound basis again. The Neo-Cons, the Obama intelligence apparat, Wall Street and the media it controls, saw in this scandal a good means of putting Trump on the defensive, so that he would not dare to seek a dialogue with Putin. The Hillary Clinton Democrats, for their part, found that "Russia-gate" provided a good way to rationalize their election defeat.

For Germany, opposing the Congress's sanctions by all means necessary, and realizing the new paradigm of the New Silk Road along with Russia and China, is a question of survival. The solution for the German economy lies in a new policy, which returns to a commitment to the general welfare, and sticks to innovation and the technologies of the future. Then it won't be necessary to use fraud to try to compete.

EIRContents

www.larouchepub.com Volume 44, Number 31, August 4, 2017

Cover This Week

Public Domain

CRUSH THE BRITISH COUP AGAINST THE PRESIDENT

Where Is All the Money Going? Bankers' Arithmetic vs. Public Credit

by Michael G. Steger

July 30—To rebuild our nation, Americans must understand what a Credit System is. The conception of a national banking system and a credit policy, or credit system, depends upon understanding the principled difference between human beings and any mere animal species. The success of a credit program, one premised on Glass-Steagall bank separation, depends upon that principled distinction, and without it, it will fail. It is not possible for any of the lower animal species to utilize a credit system. They could never do this, because a credit system is unique to the divine spark of the human individual, as applied to the broader society. Mankind is unique in its physical access to future time, as is demonstrated in what are the foreseen requirements for a young infant to become a leading scientist, artist, or generally a happy and productive member of society, when he or she one day reaches adulthood.

A credit system works because there is a unique ability for the human species to make discoveries of how—not just the visible domain functions, as we see with so-called smart phones, or biotech—but how the universe works, as seen in the gravitation discovered uniquely by Johannes Kepler. The human mind, in essence, creates entirely new features, or new dimensions—as Bernhard Riemann, the German scientist

EIRNS/Stuart Lewis

LLNL

Infrastructure in the United States (clockwise from upper left): Susquehanna nuclear power station, crop irrigation technology, inertial fusion target chamber at Lawrence Livermore National Laboratory, and the George Washington Bridge from Manhattan to New Jersey.

might say—of the universe we are actively participating in. That ability—as we see in energy technology, like nuclear power or fusion power, or in the role of economic platforms within a system of social reproduction—is the ability for mankind to participate in and transform the universe in ways no other force of nature is capable of accomplishing. To transform deserts into gardens, to transform swamps into industrial areas, to transform the Midwest into an agro-industrial heartland—these capabilities are unique to the human species.

When we invest in these areas, we get a rate of development that far exceeds anything any other species, or any other

relarustwire.com

The abandoned Carrie blast furnace in Pittsburgh, Pa.

process we know of in the universe, is capable of creating. We, as a species, transform or even create—as with nuclear fission and fusion, or a future matter/anti-matter technology—an entirely new dimension of the universe that becomes possible only through human creative discovery, as part of the lawful application of a national credit system. This is the basis for the success of a credit system, and the only means by which a society can be deemed profitable—one in which future generations have higher rates both of productivity and consumption, through the advanced reproductive platform developed via the principle of credit.

The question Americans then have to ask is: Why, fifty years ago, did we start cutting the program of credit for our nation's development? Fifty years ago, before we even got to the Moon, we cut the space program, and by the late 1970s, we had shut down all new investment into national infrastructure, manufacturing, nuclear power, education, manned space exploration, new cities, and so on. Yet, taxes and tolls continued and increased. We had money for wars in Vietnam, Panama, Nicaragua, Iraq, Afghanistan, Libya, and Syria.

Where Has All the Money Gone?

Within the United States, where has all the money gone? All this tax collection, all these bailouts?—we've been bailing out banks since the 1987 stock market crash. Alan Greenspan was brought in to bail out the failed banks after the 1987 crash. Where is all the money going?

There was a report today that Connecticut is near bankruptcy and may have to default on its public pensions. Connecticut has the highest median income in the country; it's the richest state in the country, and its entire tax base is hedge funds. There is no longer industry in Hartford or New Haven; it is all financial services, real estate, and nearly all hedge funds. And the stock market is up 20% from a year ago! So the stock market is up, and hedge funds usually make 20% when the stock market is only making 5%. The hedge funds are all located in Greenwich, Connecticut, and now they are not paying any taxes because they are all going bankrupt!

Where is all the money going?

This is the failure of money. Blame the "invisible hand" for stealing all the money! This is why a monetary system fails, because it is just money; it has no basis in what is defined as the productive powers of society—as Treasury Secretary Alexander Hamilton identified such productive powers—as the foundation for the economic success of a true nation-state republic. The Federal Reserve is lending at low, 1 to 2% interest

Vanessa S. via Twitter

The money system's underinvestment in infrastructure results: overcrowding at a New York subway station.

rates right now to Wall Street. Where is all the money going? Jamie Dimon said about eighteen months ago, "We are going to buy our own stocks!" All of the big pharmaceutical companies are buying their own stocks; it looks like everyone is buying their own stocks, and nothing much else.

They are not investing in industrial manufacturing, R&D, or machine-tool design, and they are not investing in infrastructure—just look at New York City. The entire nation is treated like a slum! These moneyed powers of Wall Street have not invested in the critical areas of society's future for nearly fifty years! What's the Port Authority in New York? What does it do with all the money on the bridges—$15 just to get into Manhattan, thousands of cars a day. Where's all the money going? Did they build new bridges, or tunnels, or subways?! None. This infrastructure is over one hundred years old in most cases. The subways are a death trap, a daily form of torture for the people of New York. People are being treated like cattle, and this is the underlying assumption of the money system— that there is no difference between human beings and the animals.

This is what a monetary system looks like. It is systemic theft. And what is it stealing? The future of our society. There is no commitment to what it means to be human.

Monetary Theft

Consider what bankers' arithmetic really is, and why this question of credit is so important: First on the principled level of what it means to be human, but then, the difference—because when you lend through public credit, you intend to create a physical change, not a monetary profit. So instead of lending to Goldman Sachs or J.P. Morgan at one percent, the way the Federal Reserve is doing today—instead, a national bank lends for the transformation of the nation's infrastructure. We need $10 trillion over the next ten years in infrastructure investment. We need a trillion over a year—not a trillion over ten years—a trillion a year, to address the slum that our nation's industry, cities, and infrastructure have become.

Consider an example: We probably need hundreds of billions just to deal with the New York City metropolitan area alone, but to take an example, let's say the nation today borrowed $10 billion to address some of the problems in New York—say, $10 billion as a number to start with. Take $10 billion borrowed at 1.5%, which is what a National Bank like the one that Alexander Hamilton set up would do today. In forty years, with the interest adding up, you would pay, at 1.5% interest rate, only $18 billion back. So for every dollar you borrow, you pay $1.80 back after forty years—and you could turn that one dollar into five or six or ten times its value by investing in a maglev rail transportation system throughout the New York City and East Coast area, and into fusion research for unlimited energy, the space program, the development of new technologies, robotics, and R&D for manufacturing with high-grade steel and new alloys—that's what our nation's credit is capable of accomplishing.

Instead, over the last thirty years, we have an economy of bubbles, otherwise known as a system of criminal fraud and theft. What the soothsayers on Wall Street call "boom and bust," is really a system of stealing. The Wall Street system reallocates the nation's credit for future generations, to a small set of Wall Street banks which serve the interest of the British Crown's Empire, with little regard for the people of the United States. As it was with Aaron Burr and J.P. Morgan, so it is with George Soros and Jamie Dimon today!

With a credit system, in forty years, we have an entirely new society and economy. By means of national credit, we reproduce the means of our society's extended future, based on the unique powers of the creative individual, and the assimilation of those discoveries into the productive powers of our society.

Now the way Wall Street runs it, they want to lend at 12%, though they get credit from the Federal Reserve at 1%! What does 12% mean? If you borrow $10 billion today, you must pay JPMorgan Chase's 12% interest rates, which is what they'll lend to a nation in Africa or to an infrastructure project in Indiana—a 12% return, if they let you borrow it for forty years at all. But if they let you borrow it for forty years, which gives you a sense of the kind of rate of return *they* expect, you would have to pay back $930 billion after forty years, i.e. nearly $1 trillion, after borrowing $10 billion. That magnitude of theft can never be paid back, so in-

New York Stock Exchange, 11 Wall Street, Manhattan.

stead, it comes in the form of cuts to education, infrastructure, the space program, health care, and so forth. This is why nations in Africa, and around the world, are still indebted to the IMF today.

This is the fascist financial system at work over these fifty years. This is why Lyndon La-Rouche intervened fifty years ago, to denounce the IMF and the British imperial system as a fascist racket, a system set to lower the level of population to less than two billion, and shut down the development of mankind.

Glass-Steagall and Public Credit

This is why Lincoln and FDR went back to Alexander Hamilton's policies, so as to develop our country at a moment of existential crisis. It is not surprising, then, that China, in 1993, adopted Glass-Steagall banking separation, just as FDR had done in 1933. Then in 1994, China set up three national banks for development and, in 1995, it expanded its entire banking system to a national credit system—and now, in the last twenty-five years, with a focus on high-tech manufacturing, nationwide industrial infrastructure platforms, fusion research, and a quickly advancing space-exploration program, China has created the greatest economic miracle mankind has ever seen—one based on the American System policies of National Credit.

This is what we can do in the United States. I think we have to do it.

Statue of Alexander Hamilton before the U.S. Treasury Building in Washington, by sculptor James Earl Fraser (1878-1853).

Hamilton's Solution to the New York City Infrastructure Crisis

by John Scialdone

July 31—The collapsing physical infrastructure of New York City is in a crisis today that can only be solved from the top, by fellow New Yorker, President Donald Trump. The current Wall Street-controlled (also from the top) monetarist approach, is like trying to stop a mudslide on the side of a mountain with picks and shovels, except that the men with the picks and shovels are actually at the top of the mountain, loading more dirt over the side. The collapse is not only outstripping the pace of all current efforts, but those efforts are self-admittedly designed to repair a system for the 1970s, at best, not the 21st Century.

Alexander Hamilton's ideas set the pace for the future of the United States: the Paterson, New Jersey works, an industrial center powered by the Passaic River.

President Trump must reintroduce the Hamiltonian principle of credit, not as a monetary mechanism, but to implement the Hamiltonian idea of *building the future, today.* Just as Hamilton attempted to design the early City of Paterson, New Jersey as a designated industrial science-city, setting the pace for the future of the United States, utilizing the Great Falls on the Passaic River as a power source—so, without a plan for what the future of New York City's water, power and transit should be fifty or more years from now, the current efforts are like trying to save a sinking ship by drilling holes in the bottom, accelerating the crisis, because the precious little time available to fix the substantially overloaded system is being squandered.

Since Alexander Hamilton breathed new life into our nation with the creation of the U.S. Constitution and the recruitment of George Washington to launch our new Republic as its first President, it has always been the case that the prin-

The driving of the ceremonial golden spike in Promontory, Utah, on May 10, 1869, that completed the nation's first transcontinental railway.

ciple of *Revolutionary Progress* for the Common Good has been the fundamental guiding principle of our nation. Indeed, Hamilton was bringing the nation back to what had already been our guiding principle since the first settlements on these western Atlantic shores.

Under the Winthrops, in the first decades of the Massachusetts Bay Colony, the first integrated iron works in history, constructed on the Saugus River, was already outproducing the best iron works of Europe. As Governor of New York State, Dewitt Clinton's Erie Canal project transformed New York City and the nation as a whole, by connecting the Eastern Seaboard to the Midwest. (As Mayor earlier, Clinton should have renamed the city Hamilton, after Hamilton was killed by British agent Aaron Burr.)

John Quincy Adams' foresight defined the United States as a continental nation—presaged by George Washington's naming his army the Continental Army—launching the rapid general expansion of road, canal and early railroad construction. Abraham Lincoln's transcontinental railroad unified the nation from east to west, even while the Civil War raged on, all the while introducing countless "Inventions and Discoveries" into the life of the nation. President Grant spread these blessings of liberty throughout the world. William McKinley—the last of the Lincoln Republicans—attempted to extend these blessings throughout the Americas. Indeed, McKinley was assassinated at the Pan-American Exposition in Buffalo, N.Y., where he was putting forward a plan for linking North, Central and South America by rail.

Franklin D. Roosevelt's Tennessee Valley Authority, Rural Electrification Program, and overall the greatest infrastructure program in history (prior to today's Belt and Road Initiative), were carried out on the back of the Wall Street/City of London induced bankruptcy of the United States. He accomplished this in the context of three Hamiltonian economic revolutions: the New Deal, the World War II mobilization, and the 1944 Bretton Woods fixed exchange-rate monetary system for his projected anti-colonial "reconstruction and development" of the post-war world.

FDR Library

Norris Dam in Tennessee, one of the Tennessee Valley Authority projects.

Eisenhower launched his Atoms for Peace program for the peaceful use of nuclear power for the development of the world; his Inter-State Highway System further integrated the nation, and his setting up of the early space program set the stage for later accomplishments. John F. Kennedy's Apollo Program took the United States and the world into space. As the plaque on the Apollo 11 lander stated, "We came in peace, for all mankind." His second administration would likely have launched the greatest water management project in history, the North American Water and Power Alliance, NAWAPA. Since his assassination by the British oligarchy and its minions within the U.S. security and intelligence establishment, our nation has gone adrift once again.

During the last fifty years, the single intervention that represented a return to Hamiltonian principles occurred when Lyndon LaRouche was brought into the picture by Ronald Reagan, with LaRouche's revolutionary approach to solving the second missile crisis, the Euro-missile crisis. This led directly to the announcing of President Reagan's Strategic Defense Initiative (SDI) program, wherein he asked the Soviet Union to join us, in asking "these great scientists who brought us weapons of mass destruction, to turn their talents now to the cause of Peace."

Thinking Too Small

So, where do we stand with respect to the current infrastructure crisis in New York? The foregoing review should already indicate what needs to be done. But two meetings that took place in the past week on the transit crisis, back to back, in Manhattan, indicate that we are instead headed for disaster. The first meeting was called by Rep. Adriano Espaillat (NY-13) in Harlem, not to present any proposals or solutions, but as an invitation to all parties involved to "come together and talk." The second meeting was the regular monthly board meeting of the Metropolitan Tranportation Authority (MTA), which had just released its plan for dealing with the transit crisis the day before.

Both of these meetings demonstrated an utter bankruptcy of ideas on the part of government leaders, as well as both a lack of vision and complete subservience to the monetarist outlook of Wall Street. Finger-pointing, useless rhetoric, and half-baked proposals were on full display.

At Congressman Espaillat's "Community Discussion on NYC Transit" on July 22, there were speakers present from the city, state and federal governments as well as several community advocacy groups, but no one from the MTA accepted the invitation to speak. Although there were Transit Workers Union (TWU) members in the audience, no one from the TWU was on the speakers list. All questions were written down and read aloud—no one was allowed to speak from the floor. Indeed, the sound system was turned up to deafening rock-concert levels throughout the hearing, making any other voice impossible to hear in any case.

Throughout the meeting, Congressman Espaillat repeatedly returned to a central theme, that there is "no use asking for more monies until there was a plan of action, and no one knows better what needs to be done than the straphangers themselves." At one point he referenced that Scott Stringer, the Comptroller, had done a survey of 1,200 NYC riders that would help provide answers. Later in the meeting, he appealed to the audience, asking them whether they would prefer a total shutdown of the lines serving the Bronx and northern Manhattan, the deepest lines in the city, for repair, as is being done with the "L" line to Brooklyn, or would they prefer "the weekend repair kind of thing?" In other words, the transit ridership was allowed to voice their opinions concerning which method of suffering they would prefer.

Similarly, most of the discussion of "Who will pay for this?" was reduced to a variety of proposals for higher taxes and tolls, that is, more looting of the population. Espaillat proposed an $8 congestion pricing for vehicles below 60th Street, proclaiming, "If people can afford to pay $40 for parking to bring their cars downtown, then they can put up $8." City Councilman Ydonis Rodriguez, chair of the NYC Transportation Committee, called for reinstating the Commuter Tax, which was repealed by Gov. Pataki in 1999, saying, "We have to put tolls into midtown." City Comptroller Scott Stringer stated, "We need a new Bond Act to finance the MTA." Assemblywoman Carmen De La Rosa, from the Governor's Transportation Committee, called for a 2% annual personal income mobility tax. The urgent need for a Lincoln/FDR-style national credit mobilization to completely rebuild the system for the 21st Century was not raised by any of the speakers.

The one subject area of the meeting in which truth made an appearance was in the depictions, given by several of the speakers, of the monumental break-down of the transit system. This included the following:

Manhattan Borough President Gale Brewer cited a *Daily News* article by the head of the TWU, saying, if the signals don't work, nothing works. The portion of the maintenance budget which goes to signal repair has dropped from 20% to 14%.

Nick Sifuentes of the Riders' Alliance, indicated that the current schedule for replacing the ancient system of signals and switches goes out to the year 2045! He also indicated that there are still subway cars running that were built in 1964, and that, of 472 stations, only 117 are wheelchair-accessible.

Scott Stringer reported that in the last twelve months, there were 981 track fires and over 20 derailments. Only 23% of stations have elevators, but they are very unreliable. In upper Manhattan, the subways go down several stories, and for many are inaccessible without elevators—which frequently break down, sometimes trapping riders inside without air conditioning or lights. In the entire NYC subway system, there are only two (two!) track cleaners! One of them is broken, and the other barely works.

On the question of "Where does the Money Go?" several speakers raised the question of auditing the MTA, including Assemblywoman De La Rosa, who stated, "The money is there, but we don't know what's happening with it. We need a line-by-line audit of the MTA." Again, all of the thinking was contained within pre-defined barriers. What should have been demanded

EIRNS/Diane Sare

Crowded 145th Street New York subway station, after a fire on the track blocked train traffic.

is a full audit of all of the Wall Street financial institutions that have looted the city dry.

Despite the rhetoric of "listening to the straphangers," all discussion at the event was tightly controlled. Only written questions were allowed, many of the questions were read but left unanswered by the speakers, and if a question was answered, follow-up questions were prohibited. In other words, there was no dialogue.

Members of the LaRouche Political Action Committee submitted two questions. The first stated the necessity to reinstate Glass-Steagall at the federal level, to purge the financial system of useless and fraudulent debt as Franklin Roosevelt had done, to be able to generate large volumes of new credit for the levels of investment required to bring the economy to a higher platform of efficiency. The second asked how the income stream from tolls and fees would ever generate the required investment if dividend payments were guaranteed, while dedicated budgets for fixed capital maintenance and improvements were not. Both questions were read, but neither was answered.

The Problems versus the Solution

A second meeting was held, on July 26, this sponsored by the MTA's Safety Committee and chaired by MTA Chairman Joe Lhota. This meeting largely consisted of horror stories about current conditions in the system.

The fruitlessness of this sort of "venting" was best characterized in a lengthy "discussion" of why there are a greater number of injuries in Penn Station than Grand Central. Apparently, it all comes down to a matter of design: Grand Central is open and spacious, while Penn Station is known for its narrow corridors and confined platforms! (Does it take the workings of a "Safety Committee" to figure out this obvious and visible reality?) At Penn Station, one never knows which track the train you are looking for will use, until a few minutes before it arrives at the platform. Then it's a mad dash, because the arriving train usually leaves within three minutes, and riders must get to the proper platform—while people in the arriving train are using the same train doors, stairs and escalators to exit. The reason for the short lead time, is that the trains themselves must wait for a platform to open up before proceeding. All this is further complicated by recurring track problems and other factors such as crew changes.

Another issue raised was the hundreds of track fires which regularly interrupt train service. A "solution" was proposed to place portable vacuum cleaners at subway platforms! The absurdity of the discussion reached an apex when one participant denounced subway riders who eat on the trains and platforms, as "pigs, pigs! They don't belong there!"

During the subsequent question-and-answer session, Diane Sare, a member of the LaRouche PAC Policy Committee, began by stating that, "We face a disaster that will cost not only millions of dollars, but the loss of human lives. The problem is Wall Street, which has turned the MTA into a debt farm, charging usurious interest rates, which necessitate more and more borrowing. Public infrastructure does not need to generate a profit at the point of use. It raises the level of productivity of the entire workforce, and therefore should be paid for through public funds and taxes. I am certain that Wall Street is not paying its fair share. Everyone in this room should demand that Glass-Steagall be re-enacted immediately, and that the President of the United States return immediately to Alexander Hamilton's program of

A CRH2E high-speed train arriving at Beijing West Railway Station.

a National Bank and Public Credit at 1% to 2% interest. Also, the Chinese Investment Corporation has just relocated from Toronto to Manhattan. It has already said that it wants to invest $50 billion in American infrastructure. China has built twenty-two thousand kilometers of high-speed rail in less than ten years—the same amount of time in which we built the Second Avenue subway. With its help and American union workers, we could completely modernize the entire metropolitan transportation grid in a shorter time than imagined by anyone in this room today. We have to stop allowing Wall Street usury to dictate infrastructure policy."

This author also addressed the Board, saying, "I'm with Lyndon LaRouche, a great economist who opposed the creation of the Municipal Assistance Corporation in the 1970s as a debt collection operation, instead of a solution to a problem at that time. And in the decades since Big MAC was created, and the MTA with it, the priority written into this thing has not been to maintain the system, but to service and collect the debt. Since the revenue coming in is never enough, what gets deferred is the maintenance,

the improvements, and the modernization; we're sitting there with a $30 billion maintenance deficit that we're now proposing to fix, which has to be fixed. I understand there have to be short-term measures because of safety, etc.—but it is not future-oriented. There's nothing here that identifies how we're going to get past this. We have foreign investment possibilities, including from China, and from Japan.

President Trump has met with these governments; they want to invest, but how can they put money into a system where the funds are used for maintaining a debt structure? There's no dedicated capital budget. It's a debt-farming operation. If it were changed, and we had a dedicated budget, there would be foreign investment, and there would be other investment. Maybe the system should be audited. Maybe there should be a moratorium on payment to bondholders until we see where the money's going and how it could be spent. My point is that we have to have a future-oriented system—not to repair a broken system, but to think about what we need twenty-five years from now, and fifty years from now. We should start building that now, in the context of solving the problem."

Later, Jessica White, a recently retired NYC public-

Xinhua

A track-laying vehicle lays the last section of steel rail on the western ring of the high-speed rail loop line, in south China's Hainan Province, June 30, 2015.

school science teacher spoke: "I'm here to say. with all due respect to every MTA worker and my fellow union workers, there is no reason to pit police against riders, or riders against MTA workers, or workers against the city, or the city against the state. The city of New York has been eaten alive by Wall Street and City of London looting operations. This is true also for cities outside of New York. Take a look at Detroit. City officials have also been taking kickbacks from Wall Street, and you know what I'm talking about, you in the audience. These kickbacks from Wall Street extend all the way into Congress and into our Senate, even in Washington, D.C. This money that Gov. Cuomo is referring to will end up on the backs of the people of this city, sooner rather than later.

"We need to crush Wall Street by reinstating the Glass-Steagall act. This Glass-Steagall Act is the first of Lyndon LaRouche's 'Four Laws.' This Act was deliberately taken down in 1999. It was actually tantamount to treason, because of the collapse of the legitimate banking system, which is commercial banking, in favor of the speculating wolves on Wall Street. An imminent collapse of the entire trans-Atlantic banking system is hanging over our heads, with a derivatives bubble of $1.5 quadrillion, which cannot conceivably be sustained, even if Social Security, Medicare, and Medicaid are all wiped out at the same time. What we need to do, and you on this board—I challenge you—is to tell your Congress people to reinstate Glass-Steagall, to allow the credit of the U.S. to go to the states. That will put infrastructure projects online just as it brought us out of the Depression. Those infrastructure projects will save our lives. Glass-Steagall will pay for that. This is a bipartisan bill, HR 790, which is already in Congress. It's been there for a while. We need to reinstate Glass-Steagall, and everybody in this room needs to tell their Congressman to do so, to fund this infrastructure project and other lifesaving projects for NYC. Thank you."

Build Big with Hamilton

As Diane Sare said, China has built 22,000 km of high-speed rail in the same ten years that NYC has

Hangzhou Metro Line 1. By 2019 the subway network will be further enlarged with six metro lines, totaling about 190 km.

taken to build the Second Avenue subway. Actually, the Second Avenue line was started in 1972, but stopped in 1975 by Felix Rohatyn and Richard Ravitch's Big MAC, on behalf of Wall Street. And still today, the Second Avenue line is not even near completion; only phase one has been completed, with three stops between 96th Street and the 63rd Street, connecting there with the BMT Broadway line. Phases two and three of the original plan will take it from 125th Street down to Hanover Square in lower Manhattan—just past Wall Street. Fewer than twenty years ago, China had subway systems in only three cities, Beijing, Shanghai and Guangzhou. Today, China has subway systems in twenty-five cities, all with populations of three million or more. Now they are moving on to cities with populations as little as 1.5 million.

As Diane Sare also said, infrastructure is not paid for by collecting tolls at the point of service. That only makes the system less efficient. It is paid for in the increased tax revenue accrued through the benefit of the infrastructure for the improvement of the nation as a whole. China replaced their universal banking system in 1975, with a Glass-Steagall banking system, identifying FDR's original Glass-Steagall bank separation law as a model at the time.

Alexander Hamilton's writings are well known in China. His principles have guided the modernization of many nations, including Germany, Russia, Japan and others. Let's do it right, the way Hamilton would do it. What are we waiting for?

Russian 'Hacking'—Truth versus Lies

The following is an edited version of the LaRouche PAC International Webcast from June 28. The host was Jason Ross of LaRouche PAC, and the webcast contained excerpts of an interview, by Ross, with Ray McGovern of the Veterans Intelligence Professionals for Sanity (VIPS). Also speaking was Diane Sare of the LaRouche Policy Committee.

Jason Ross: My name is Jason Ross, and I'm glad you're joining us for the Friday LaRouche PAC webcast. We're going to be covering an issue today that's of the greatest importance for the nation. I have on the show with me this week Diane Sare, who's joining us from our Manhattan Project in New York.

The issue that concerns us today is that of "Russia-gate." We have heard so often, and there has been so much said, about the "irrefutable" supposed evidence that Donald Trump was placed in the White House by the machinations of Vladimir Putin, that it's almost taken as a given. Everyone assumes it happened; in fact, it was written into the Russian sanctions bill that just passed the House and the Senate, as an assumption, that we know Vladimir Putin put Trump into office; that Putin ordered an influence campaign on the U.S. election. It's not true.

The VIPS Memo

This week, on Monday, the Veteran Intelligence Professionals for Sanity released a memo called, "Was the 'Russian Hack' an Inside Job?" In it, they demolish the central claim of the entire Russia-gate story. That central claim is that Russian hackers were involved in getting material from the Democratic National Committee, material that was very embarrassing towards Hillary Clinton, and

releasing it via Wikileaks. This hinges on the central character of the Internet persona known as Guccifer 2.0, and the intelligence committee assessment which came out January 6, 2017 at the very end of the Obama administration. This is the report that everybody has been citing, that supposedly all of the intelligence agencies agree with this assessment. It's not true. Only a hand-picked group of intelligence agencies were involved in that assessment at all, and their assessment is not unanimous. That central evidence factor is what we're going to be talking about today in terms of this VIPS memo.

We had the good fortune to be able to interview one of the founding members of the Veteran Intelligence Professionals for Sanity, Ray McGovern, who is a former very top level analyst at the CIA, who during his career, had prepared Presidential daily briefs for the President. Last night we asked him if he could lay out what the implications are of the memo that they put forward, and here's what he had to say:

LaRouche PAC's Jason Ross (left) interviews Ray McGovern of the Veteran Intelligence Professionals for Sanity.

Ray McGovern: The 12th of June, 15th of June? As soon as they learned that Julian Assange had emails related to Hillary Clinton, "What are you going to do?" Well, as I reconstruct it—"What we do is, we say, 'It's from the Russians.'" So, CrowdStrike, which was working for the DNC, announces, "There's malware, and we think it was the Russians." Then immediately, the same day, Guccifer says "Yeah, yeah! We did it, and we're working for Julian Assange."

Now, this is how we interpret it: the idea was "since Julian Assange was going to come out with emails, God knows when, maybe right before the Democratic National Convention—my God, that would be awful. So, we'll say he got it from the Russians, and that way we can divert attention from what's in the emails; because God knows how much he's got there, he might be able to show that we stole the nomination from Bernie Sanders! It's probably in there, you know? So, let's do this little pre-emptive move—in June, before he ever gets this stuff out." Julian doesn't adulterate these things, what he does is array them in searchable form. "It's going to take a while. So, we have a little time, about six weeks or so,"—they didn't know how long—"but let's do it right away." So, when Julian Assange comes out with this, they're all set to say, "Ah ha! It was the Russians hacking."

A Magnificent Diversion

Now this was a magnificent—I remember the old movie or book, *Magnificent Obsession*,— this was magnificent diversion. Because as soon as Julian Assange outed the emails related to Hillary Clinton—that was on the 22nd of July, three days before the Democratic National Convention began—they were prepared. They were prepared to say "Ah ha! Russia did it! Russia did it!" You can see them sort of sitting around a table. Here's Hillary saying "My God! What are we going to do? What will Bernie say? He's already said he'd acquiesce, but what will he say now?" Somebody says, "I know what we do. We'll blame the Russians." "But it wasn't the Russians, it was Julian Assange." "That's all right. We'll say that Julian Assange was working for the Russians." "Yeah, but what's the rationale?" "Oh, come on! The Russians want Trump to win, because Trump has said nice things about Putin; this is going to be easy to prove. Anybody got any better

Former Secretary of State Hillary Clinton.

wikimedia

ideas?" "OK, let's go with that." It worked beautifully. The mainstream media played the story.

Ross: Just to offer this chronology for our viewers, because this has become so shrouded in the mists of time that it's sort of hard to take the pieces of it apart, to repeat, in June 2016, Julian Assange, the Wikileaks founder, announced that he had received material from the DNC and that he was going to be releasing it. Within a matter of days, the DNC's IT firm, CrowdStrike, announced that they had proof that Russia had hacked their computers. Also, an Internet hacker calling himself Guccifer 2.0 appeared out of nowhere, saying that he was the hacker, he got into the DNC's system, and he says, "I'll prove it. Here's some of the material that I stole." In June, documents were released by this Guccifer person that included the most obvious ham-fisted fake clues you've ever seen. These documents were deliberately altered in order to incorporate—in Cyrillic— "Felix Edmundovich" as the document's last editor. Now, Felix Edmundovich Dzerzhinsky was the founder of the Soviet secret police. You might think that if Russian hackers are doing something, they might not be so obvious as to label themselves on their computers with that name; it's just an obvious fake clue to be found. Additional proof supposedly came up in Guccifer 2.0 trying to hide his persona, pretending to be Romanian while not really speaking Romanian, so that people could say "Ah ha! He's hiding his identity. We found these total clues"—really red herrings—"of these Russian names inside the documents. The documents were set to the language of Russia. Ah ha! This is proof."

Now what it really means is that those documents were artificially altered. That's what the Veteran Intelligence Professionals for Sanity go through in this memorandum called, "Was the 'Russian Hack' an Inside Job?" So, as Mr. McGovern said, following this, a large release of documents came from Guccifer sometime in September. These documents, according to forensic analysis that's been reviewed by the Veteran Intelligence Professionals for Sanity, reveals that the documents were not hacked, but they were leaked, they were copied. The rate of data transmission, the rate of the file creation, indicates a speed that exceeds what you would possibly be able to get over the Internet if you had hacked into a computer and then pulled the files out. They reason, then, that this indicates that these files were simply copied, and then put out tainted with this Guccifer 2.0 persona to give a sense of Russian involvement in the hacking. The fact of the matter is that *no evidence whatsoever has ever been presented that can show where Wikileaks got its material*. The founder of Wikileaks, Julian Assange, said this was a leak, it was not a hack. It didn't come from Russia, it didn't come from a Russian state actor. It was a leak. As Mr. McGovern said, there were plenty of people in the DNC who weren't very happy about the way that the primary elections were handled. There is plenty of motive for a leak to put out the truth about how the DNC had operated.

Anti-Russia Hysteria

But on top of this fabricated evidence, we now have a situation where this anti-Russia hysteria is phenomenal. Just yesterday, we had the passage of an anti-Russia sanctions bill through the House and through the Senate. This bill, HR 3364, takes as a given that Russia hacked the U.S. elections, imposes very strong sanctions in a variety of cases, and forbids the President from changing them. In other words, it takes away the ability of the President, in this case President Trump, to initiate foreign policy, which is, frankly, part of the President's job. That's the way we work in this country.

One of the most shocking things about all of this is that this supposed Russian "hacking" has been called an Act of War by numerous members of Congress. People

Fake proof: "Russia" in Cyrillic, conveniently embedded in code.

say that because of this, Donald Trump should be impeached; this has been said by members of Congress. For something of this magnitude, an act of war leading to sanctions and the potential break-out of conflict with the world's most powerful nuclear power besides ourselves, surely a good investigation would have been done. Well, it wasn't! As a matter of fact, after the DNC computers were supposedly hacked, who investigated them? Not the FBI—but a private firm, CrowdStrike, with political ties that make its findings very suspicious.

The Veteran Intelligence Professionals for Sanity ended their memo by questioning who Guccifer 2.0 is. They say, "Maybe you should ask the FBI." So, I asked Ray McGovern, "Why might we want to ask the FBI?"

McGovern: After it was revealed that the DNC had been "hacked," so to speak, normally what would happen in that case, unless I'm sadly mistaken, would be that the FBI would be invited in to take a look and see who did this. Or, the DNC would say "Would you please come in here and see who did this?" But you know what? Neither seemed to be very interested in looking at that. So, with all due respect, and not much is due, really, James Comey is guilty of malfeasance, not just misfeasance. People crying that this is an act of war, and he sits back and says "I don't want to send my technicians in there." Why? Well, I can tell you why. It seems to me that when you're an intelligence analyst, you have this kind of bent to connect dots; that's what we call an "all-source analyst." You look not only at the technical details, the forensics, now that we have them, but what was going on outside, what you learn from the newspapers. And we know from that, that the CIA, with the help of the NSA, had developed—it took them fifteen years—an incredible capability.

Ross: That capability that McGovern is referring to,

"Hacked " DNC computers were investigated by—not the FBI—but CrowdStrike. Right: Former Director of the FBI, James Comey.

fbi.gov

is what was revealed in March under the program of Vault 7, which was released from Wikileaks. One aspect of that was called the Marble Framework; something developed by the CIA that made it possible to obfuscate the origins of cyber attacks. In other words, the CIA had spent a tremendous amount of effort—Mr. McGovern estimates billions of dollars being spent—to develop the ability to perform hacks, and then to be able to attribute them to other nations, to other actors. He says that this Marble Framework allowed the CIA to deliberately plant fake evidence of Russian involvement. They had Cyrillic text that could be inserted; in other words, it would be possible to make it look as though attackers were coming from Russia. Now the question would be, has this been investigated? Has Trump taken up with his intelligence agencies, an investigation to find out if these types of capabilities were used? Mr. McGovern says that it was revealed that they were used in 2016. Was this their use? An investigation would be able to show that.

This also raises the question, why the animosity towards Russia? Is this a cynical campaign ploy by the Democrats to get over an election that they lost and try to impeach Trump, to try and take back control of the country? Or what else is at play here? Why would this sanctions bill pass so unanimously, with only three House members voting against it, and only two Senators? Well, we asked Ray McGovern what he thought about this:

McGovern: It's coming mostly from the Democrats, curiously enough. And initially, as I tried to explain before, it was an attempt to blacken the Russians to help Hillary become elected. Then, when she wasn't elected, "Whoops! We can still use this stuff. How can we use it? To show that Hillary didn't lose the election; it couldn't have been that she was not such a good candidate, or that nobody trusted her. It's the Russians!" So, most Americans now believe—according to the polls—that this fellow Trump who we have as Presi-

dent now, is there because of Vladimir Putin helping him become elected. That's bad! That's really bad.

What's the objective now? Well, the objective is not only to de-legitimize Trump, but to keep the tensions stoked with Russia so that there can be no real detente; so that we can blacken the Russians and say, "Oh, look!"

Ross: Now, the other objective, or the other incident that caused all of this Russia hysteria, was what occurred in Ukraine, where a coup carried out in 2014 overthrew the elected President of Ukraine, Viktor Yanukovych, and instituted a new government. United States involvement in this coup was as clear as day. Those of us who were watching, saw on YouTube the videos covering the audio recordings, with American officials planning out what the new Ukrainian government would be. We had [Assistant Secretary of State] Victoria Nuland involved in helping to set up a new government in Ukraine. In reaction to the coup, when the people of Crimea voted democratically to rejoin Russia, the same people said, "We will never have peace with Russia until Russia returns Crimea to Ukraine; the sanctions will continue. Russia is everybody's enemy."

Keeping that in mind, that it was *U.S. interference* in Ukraine that created the destabilization in the Ukraine, leading eventually to Crimea's rejoining with Russia, we can ask ourselves, "Where is this going if this process isn't stopped?" Here's what Mr. McGovern had to say about that:

Where Is This Going?

McGovern: Put all this together, you've got a synthetic,— you've got a kind of an artificial construct of Vladimir Putin as the Devil Incarnate. The whole press does this meme, and everybody catches on, especially the Democrats, and it's the oddest thing I've ever seen. So, here's Donald Trump; he wants to go and talk to Putin. Everybody says "Oh, this is really bad." He does talk to Putin, and what happens? They get a cease-fire agreement! It's not the whole thing, but a little slice of Syria. Does that get reported in the press? No, maybe an inside page.

Ross: They say it's giving in to Russia.

McGovern: So, if any of us have any interest in stopping the carnage in Syria, which we should, we should applaud Trump or any other effort to work with the other forces in play, not only the Russians, but the Syrians, the Turks, and the Iranians. If we don't have a common aim against ISIS, what do we have a common aim against?

What's going to be interesting right now—Trump this week decided no more support, no more arms or money for the so-called "moderate" rebels, the rebels that the U.S. has supported in Syria. That's big! That's the CIA's bag; that's billions of dollars invested in that. What's going to happen? Well, Trump has taken on the CIA on that issue. And what I'm recalling now is—nobody's been around in Washington as long as Senator Chuck Schumer, the ranking Democrat in the Senate, and in a recent interview [Jan. 3, 2017] with Rachel Maddow, this is what he said:

Rachel Maddow: He's taking these shots and antagonisms—

Chuck Schumer: Yup.

Maddow: —taunting the intelligence agencies.

Schumer: Let me tell you; you take on the intelligence community, they have six ways from Sunday at getting back at you.

McGovern: Rachel Maddow says, "Oh, we're going to go to break." Give me a break! If it were you, wouldn't you say, "Are you saying that the President of the United States should be afraid of the intelligence community?" Of course, that's what he was saying. So, why do I refer to that? The jury is out. He's taken them on a little bit. Whether he'll take them on on the "Russian hack"—well I don't know. Maybe [CIA Director] Pompeo is afraid to ask these guys; or maybe *he's* afraid to ask. If he's afraid, well he's following the example of his predecessor [Obama], because Obama was deathly afraid of Brennan; that's why he defended him when Brennan hacked into the Senate computers. That's why he tried to prevent the publication of the memo from the Senate on CIA torture; because it showed that Brennan and the others had been lying through their teeth about the effectiveness of torture techniques. So Obama was very much defending himself or defending them, ultimately to defend themselves. So, whether Schumer is right, we're likely to see sooner rather than later.

Ross: We'll find out sooner rather than later based on how the President and how the American population respond to this pressure. Think for a minute in your mind: What would it mean if Trump were thrown out of office based on what we know to be a fabrication, a lie created by the intelligence agencies, a lie saying that Vladimir Putin put him in office? If the President of the United States can be removed from office based on nonsense created by the intelligence agencies, do we have elected government in the United States? I think that that's the question that we need to take up in a very urgent way by getting out the explosive news about this memo coming from the Veteran Intelligence Professionals for Sanity.

Mobilizing to Break the Story

Diane Sare: We are going to ask everybody watching this program to mobilize to break this story. I first want to address some of the questions that people may raise: "Of course we know the Russians didn't hack the election. I voted for Trump, and I wasn't told to vote for Trump by Vladimir Putin. So, what's new about this?" Or people say, "We're used to being lied to all the time. Why does this make a difference?"

I want to say a little bit about who some of these people are. In case you missed it, Ray McGovern is a former U.S. Army and former CIA intelligence agent; I believe he is fluent in Russian and has a great deal of knowledge on this. Bill Binney, who is the co-author of this report, is the former NSA Technical Director for World Geopolitical and Military Analysis, the co-founder of the NSA Signals Intelligence Automation Research Center—that is the data-mining. He designed, in part, the technology to be able to spy on everyone; he knows it very well. The expert who did the forensics on these so-called hacks, which turned out to be a leak, is someone named Skip Holden, who's a retired IBM Program Manager for Information Technology. He's the one who looked at this, who came to the conclusion that there was no hack, that what happened was that 1,976 megabytes of data were copied in only 87 seconds, which cannot be done over the Internet. That cannot be done through cyberspace, but only by using some kind of thumb drive, USB port, some kind of storage device that is actually inserted into the computer to copy this data. And that this was done by someone operating in the Eastern U.S. time zone. Then this was blamed on Russia.

We have in hand, in this report, by a group of certified experts, proof, the documentation that this thing is a fraud from the beginning. That is extremely important. Yesterday four LaRouche organizers went to Congress to distribute about 1,000 copies of the VIPS report, and discovered that nobody there had heard anything about this; which is outrageous. You might remember, before the elections, that President Obama and others had promised there was going to be a classified briefing for the Congress, presenting the alleged proofs that the Russians were hacking into the Democratic Party and sabotaging the elections, and then such briefing never occurred. There never was any evidence presented.

Victoria Nuland, the State Department expert on how to make color revolution coups, hands out buns in Kiev's Maidan Square, as U.S. Ambassador to Ukraine Geoffrey Pyatt looks on, December 2013.

LaRouche's Assessment

I just want to take a step back for a second, because when Lyndon LaRouche heard about Comey's testimony and the story about Russia, he said, "The people pushing this want thermonuclear war. If they succeed, we're going to have thermonuclear war with Russia." I'd like to remind people that what happened in Ukraine was a direct result of a deliberate policy, as Jason said. They violently overthrew the government with $5 billion, largely from George Soros, laundered through the U.S. State Department. Victoria Nuland was under Hillary Clinton as Secretary of State. In other words, we were provoking war with Russia, deliberately moving NATO eastward, putting Nazis—actual supporters of Hitler and Stepan Bandera—in power in Ukraine on Russia's border. Why? Because the transAtlantic system is on the brink of total disintegration. The British Empire, this empire monarchy, is in its final agony; it will not survive. They've printed trillions of dollars, they've bailed out the banks time and again, they've created a gigantic bubble; it's going down.

The same thing in Syria: People may remember, Hillary Clinton was proposing a no-fly zone over Syria so that we could shoot down Russian planes in defense of ISIS. As Ray McGovern mentioned in the interview, one of the positive developments of the Trump Presidency, a very significant one, is he met with Putin, got a ceasefire, and we are no longer arming the so-called "moderate" groups who are running around chopping people's heads off and filming it. It's a huge breakthrough.

So, I just want to underscore the fact that we have in our hands, by a group of highly competent professionals, the proof that the entire story about Russia hacking the elections was a fraud. Russia did not start the violence in Ukraine; that was launched under Victoria Nuland with funding from George Soros and the State Department. It's a bunch of Nazis. Russia did not "illegally annex" Crimea. The people of Crimea, who are predominantly Russian and Russian speaking, held a referendum where they voted to leave Ukraine so they wouldn't be burned to death in buildings for speaking Russian, which is what these Nazis did to people in Odessa, for example. There was a legitimate vote in Crimea.

When Assange's evidence came out, Putin said, "Why are people so concerned? You should be concerned that what was leaked was actually true," which was that the Hillary Clinton campaign had ripped off Bernie Sanders in every imaginable way, and there was nothing honest or up-front about the way she conducted her campaign. People suspected it, and that was then proven. People remember that Wasserman-Schultz had to resign.

What we are asking you to do is several things. One, the Congress should stop being a bunch of sold-out, gutless wonders, and they should hold hearings with the actual evidence. That is, Ray McGovern, Bill Binney, Skip Holden—they should all be invited to testify in hearings in the Congress. You can call into the Congressional switchboard, which is (202) 224-3121. People can also sign and circulate the petition available on the LaRouche PAC website. As I mentioned, what we discovered in Washington is that no one had even heard of this report. We have to change the so-called narrative; that's one thing that we've run into in D.C. Everyone talks about narrative this, narrative that, as if there's no such thing as truth. Well, the narrative right now is that somehow Vladimir Putin is responsible for every evil that's occurred on the planet in the last ten years at least, and that therefore, we should impose sanctions on Russia and even risk a war with that nation. This is completely insane; it is not true. The truth of the matter is that there is a New Paradigm which is being led by China, in which the U.S. can join with China and Russia. It has the potential, as President Trump has expressed his intent, to make American great again. The way we make America great again is by collaborating with China, with Russia, to go back to a Hamiltonian system of political economy.

We have to get the truth out on this story. The Veteran Intelligence Professionals for Sanity (VIPS), have given us a weapon. What we want to do with this mobilization is break the back of this lie. The American people have been lied to for a very long time. We were lied to about the Kennedy assassination with devastating consequences to our republic. We were lied to about 9/11; we were lied to about the Saudi and British role in 9/11 explicitly. We are now being lied to about the election, and these lies could have the consequence of running a coup d'etat against a legitimately elected leader and putting us on a trajectory for World War III. We can break the back of this by circulating this report.

I would urge people to take the material from the LaRouche PAC website, get it out on your Facebook accounts, send it out through Twitter. Call the White House and urge President Trump to appoint special

Former CIA Director John Brennan.

counsel to launch a Presidential investigation of what happened in the DNC computers. As Ray McGovern asked, "What does the CIA know about this? What does Brennan know about this? What does the FBI know about this? Who was it who went into the DNC computer and tried to make it look like Russia had done this?" President Trump, as President of the United States, has a legitimate right to demand such an investigation. You should call the White House and demand this. Call your Congressman and say, "Have you read the report from the Veteran Intelligence Professionals for Sanity? Have you read that report? Don't you think there should be hearings? We have to investigate this." Get this out to all of your friends; it's absolutely urgent. Because when we break the back of this, then we can transform the nation.

It is very important that people take action. The LaRouche PAC website will be the center of this mobilization, giving you the ammunition that you need and the resources that you need to get to your elected officials.

Do You Want to Have a Government?

Ross: I just want to bring up one more aspect of this in terms of the coup. Diane brought up John Brennan. Well, John Brennan, at the Aspen Security Forum just a couple of days ago, said that if Trump fires Robert Mueller, the special investigator, that the intelligence agencies should refuse to go along with it. In essence, he's calling for a coup against the President, based on a political decision that he might make. So, ask yourself: Do you want to have a government? Or do you want to have John Brennan and other unelected people dictating and determining policy in a way that is to the absolute detriment of our nation? Get that memo out; make sure everybody you know reads it. It's absolutely dynamite, and it definitively puts to rest the whole Russiagate nonsense. It'll be great to move on from that, won't it?

Thank you for joining us. I'm looking forward to your action to make this a reality.

NOVEMBER 29, 2010

Reflections on a Work by Nicholas of Cusa: The Strategic Situation Now

by Lyndon H. LaRouche, Jr.

Foreword

Let this be said, with the same intention with which I had named that poem of mine from sixty years ago, "My Lyre." It were as a universe which that poetic spirit within me had described as "bending stars like reeds."

Now, during the recent lapse of time since the Spring of this year 2011, I had devoted myself, largely, to working through successive stages of the continuing theme of this present year's series of pieces of mine, of which one major title (the present one) is still currently in progress at this moment. This series, when it will have been taken in its whole, has a single, commonly subsuming theme, with a virtually completed discovery as presented in this published version sent to print.

Yet, this has also been a fairly well-defined mission which had been in the process of continuous resolution into its early expression since the first steps during the post-war 1940s, under the ruinous practices of President Harry S Truman and putative economist Arthur Burns, throughout the 1945-1960 interval, and into the incarnation it has acquired during the recent weeks. During the greater part of the recent eight months, I had been in the process of defining what has now become a uniquely competent method for defining the means for securing general physical-economic growth. My intention during the longer period from 1956-57, and beyond, had been to establish my competence in what had already become the early rudiments of an inherently successful, new method for long-ranging economic forecasting and policy-design, a competence which has since developed into becoming the most ef-

fective economic policy-shaping doctrine known publicly today.

What I had accomplished had been a process of ongoing discoveries which had taken shape, and had continued through, and beyond my early 1950s' focus on the theme of Bernhard Riemann's 1854 habilitation dissertation. So, inspirations, like dreams, return to appear as the harvests of successive years.

So, when I had just returned to the United States from military service in Asia, in the Spring of 1946, I settled into experiencing the economic problems of both the post-World War II world, and what came to be known as "The Cold War." As we were to discover when President John F. Kennedy would have been assassinated, the fact was that with the assassination of President Kennedy, this nation was no longer really what our republic has been under such as Franklin Roosevelt, Dwight Eisenhower and John F. Kennedy, but one which had been largely taken over by our enemies, the British Empire and its subaltern known in street-slang as "Wall Street."

Those of our citizens who still do not understand that set of facts, do not really know where their own identity lies. That fact shows itself in nearly every aspect of the lives of our citizenry today. In short, the condition of actually being free, begins with knowing what it is from which one must be freed. There are almost no truly free citizens in our United States, or most of Europe, today; as much as a margin of former freedom still exists, it is presently vanishing at an accelerating rate under the nominal authority of the succession of U.S. President George W. Bush, Jr., and has now almost vanished under the term of a carbon-copy of the Roman Emperor Nero, the British royal puppet, U.S. President Barack Obama.

If we are to become freed again, as Martin Luther King had said, "free at last," freed from the evil practices of virtual British puppets such as President George W. Bush, Jr., and Barack Obama, we must understand the essential facts concerning our republic's present situation, and recognize how this presently wretched, virtual decade came about, and how that horrid result might be cured.

To that end, as I remind you now, the individual composition which I present here, is a particular element in a continued batched series of related utterances by me, since the now past Spring of this year. There is also a deeper aspect, even in essential elements deep in history, which are urgently to be reawakened for consideration, for reflection here, now, while I walk with you, the reader, through that experience, in this report, here.

This process on which I shall report here, is one which reaches back, from that which might often seem to have been scattered recollections, but which, now, must become a more prominently featured, and much-matured subject of discussions, such as those discussions published under the impact of my present attention to such continuing, present-day concerns, as they appear to me today. Therefore, I report here on the subject of the ontological implications of the same Classical perspective which had also been already expressed, relatively long ago, by a succession of such exceptional ancient minds as since Heraclitus and Plato.

That recurring experience of ancient through present-day history has been, for me, truly an ancient concern, a concern which is currently expressed for me

"If we are to become free again, as Martin Luther King had said, 'free at last,' freed from the evil practices of virtual British puppets such as President George W. Bush, Jr., and Barack Obama, we must understand the essential facts concerning our republic's present situation, and recognize how this presently wretched, virtual decade came about, and how that horrid result might be cured."

more and more forcefully as I become older. These concerns have been expressed in publications, especially those of my own and of a rare few others. I refer to those others who are devoted to the subject of the present terms of my ever-more-revolutionary definition of the appropriate, ontological basis and design for the needed reform in scientific method for economy, as for today. It is not my advancing age, as such, which defines that difference; it is the ever-more-menacing condition which has already been reached now, a condition of general trans-Atlantic economic breakdown on this planet: a condition which has presently reached a critical point as has happened within the recent several days. Your world, and mine, has now entered a qualitatively new stage of history, which should be regarded as the end-stage of an entire period of history, an end-stage which is presently closing in upon us with a deadly grip; but, hopefully, it is also the forewarning of the opportunities for a new, better age very soon to begin.

This is a time, not for reporting events, even merely important events; it is time to launch an entirely new quality in world history. So, in the pages of this report, I must report matters here, with that intention, accordingly.

Percy Shelley & History

When I take into account what I am proud to have accomplished in the course of such a presently continued undertaking as that, up to this time, I must insist, that the original inspiration for this project of mine, is still exemplified in spirit, by the celebrated, concluding paragraph of Percy Bysshe Shelley's **A Defence of Poetry**. On that account, nothing has been left "worn out."

Sometimes, as in some persons' reading of Shelley's concluding paragraph for his **A Defence of Poetry**, there had been suspicion expressed by some, that Shelley had left that poem uncompleted. That poem and I have both proven to have been wiser than to permit such a conclusion; in the end, we, of my dedication, have understood that Shelley had ended this work on that publication at the stage when his actual intention in writing that report had been fulfilled by him, and for him, at that point. We must recognize that he had completed his statement made, implicitly to you, on that occasion; it is now your turn—for each of us—to respond to him; have you succeeded in responding with a relevant, decent quality of reaction of your own?

The categorically ontological feature of the course of my own first study of Shelley's composition, a composition which was originally uttered by him about two centuries ago, has left an effect on me which I had experienced repeatedly in the course of both my adolescence, and my adult years to date. Each time I had read Shelley's **A Defence of Poetry**, especially since the immediate post-World War II period, I had come away with an always refreshed expression and in greater strength of conviction. This experience has become an effect on me which may be located in respect to the beautiful temptation which should have been what had aroused Shelley's admirers then (as it certainly did a few). The actual principle of his work, whose internal reality I had discovered on my own account, has now enabled me to report that fact to you, here, and now, in this refreshed, present expression; it is now also expressed for me as a fact which had existed on its own account, as a principle, such as Shelley's own, even long before I had been actually born. We are each, after all, the victim of our parents' generation, and, also, our own.

What I have done, for my part, in this still-ongoing evolution of that maturing drama, is to have brought you, the reader, to a point of confrontation with my own original, living insights into that principle; so, in this manner, I shall now confront you, as I do in this present report. I confront you, with the challenge of your obligation to share my own, still ever-deepening insight into the subject-matter of the ontological implications of the physical notion of what is to be recognized presently, here. I present that as my notion of the principle of the universality of the truly physical principle of metaphor.

Shelley's Method

As for Shelley's notion itself, classical irony were never a thing unto itself; it were better said, that such ironies as those, are typical of the same relevant points which are to be traced to such as, for example, such English poets as Shakespeare and Shelley. It is the fundamental principle of **irony**, the rarely recognized, true meaning of the physical principle called **metaphor**, which remains, still today, as belonging in very significant part, to the specifically ontological implications of the work of both of those great poets.

For the sake of irony, my native language is, admittedly, English. It is, most emphatically, the American English descended from what had once been the proudly literate region of the New England coast since the founding of New England early during the Seventeenth Century. Nonetheless, I have based my argument here, as I must say, "prudently," such that it includes such European influences as have been expressed, chiefly, as fruits of the tradition passed down to me as it had been created by the greatest English and German poets known to me as those who had lived since, whether sooner or later, in the sunlight and shadows cast by the leaders of the Fifteenth-century Renaissance, for whom my own preferred choice of reference is, for me, their relevance as means for illustrating the true discovery of my America. The principle of metaphor, is not merely physically supreme, but it also reflects the spiritual qualities of their intentions as my own, and that with conceptions such as those which I present as a report of that result in this present publication.

To a certain degree, it might seem to me now, as to some others, that, at the least, my subject here almost speaks for itself. However, I must not only admit, but insist from the outset, that it does not, and could not actually speak for itself; "seems" or "almost," is not "actual."

It is therefore necessary, for my purpose here, that we share this present statement among us with the accompanying assumption that we might wish that the matter were able, at the least, to seem to speak for itself. In fact, sadly, it does not do that, and could not. So, with such reservations taken into account, we might be enabled to adduce the higher wisdom presented to us by the stubbornness of a discovery of that which, in this connection, does not actually speak to us directly for itself, but impels me to work to discover what had not been otherwise revealed.

The great error which needs to be removed from our

"I have based my argument here . . . in the sunlight and shadows cast by the leaders of the Fifteenth-Century Renaissance, for whom my own preferred choice of reference is their relevance as means for illustrating the true discovery of my America." The principle of metaphor: "St. Peter Healing with His Shadow," Masaccio (1426); the Brancacci Chapel, Florence.

of some foolish students (or professors) of physical science, like those university students, or graduates who failed to comprehend the unique genius of both Johannes Kepler's uniquely original discovery of the actual principle of universal gravitation, as a student who, therefore, lacked insight into the implications of Kepler's great, unique discovery of the true principle of gravitation, a discovery which is also highly relevant in respect to the physical principle which is our subject here. I also mean the implications bearing on the method expressed by the crucially distinct, specific contributions of such later exemplars of science as Bernhard Riemann, Max Planck, Albert Einstein, and Academician V.I. Vernadsky, as considered in that order.

What Is Metaphor?

I am aware, in a general fashion, of a rather large proportion among those who have acquired a "classroom" sort of apparently literate, but, nonetheless, intellectually failed sort of presumed familiarity with the proper import of the term "metaphor." Of these, a few exceptional persons may even have actually acquired a certain kind of "look-it-up-in-the-back-of-the-book" literacy in the conventional use of the term "metaphor;" but, only a tiny minority among those persons, commands an actually competent insight into the distinctive, strict meaning, and the real significance of what might regarded as the strictly scientific meaning of the Classical "actor" in the Classical drama. I mean one who, himself, fits the standard of metaphor.

A strict meaning of the term "metaphor," does not refer to a particular, explicitly direct object, or set of objects; it refers, to an implied simultaneity among a very special quality of several, indirectly related objects.

Consider the case of such an apparent characteristic of such a shadow-like object cast as such a pair, or, more. In such cases we are able to conceptualize the specific effect which accounts for the generation of the shadow of such a pair-wise, or comparable shadow; but we do not "see" the relevant sort of linkage among those considerations which pertain to that which has been either a pair of shadows, or some larger set of such

mutual considerations between you, the reader, and me, the writer, is to be blamed largely on the cruelly fraudulent, self-inflicted presumptions of the perennially credulous. Blame the folly of the proverbial "true believer": blame the absurdity of the presumption that "truth" lies within the proverbial bounds of "sense certainty."

Worst of it all, is the credulous victim's all too typical, ontological presumption, which is his, or her belief in the actual existence of what is conventionally described as "empty space." Similarly, there is the belief an array, as might be defined by named "characters." Functionally, we do not "see" the actual object; the real character is actually performed, not on the stage (even if one were there); it lies in the idea implanted in the minds of the audience viewing the performing actor, or actors; this is to be recognized, not by vision, but as to be seen within the mind of the viewing audience, rather than a projection on a linear screen. It can not be seen with the mere eyes and ears of the audience, but only by means of the superior potentialities of that power of the human mind which creates the images of those person-alities called to the mind of the audience by means of a higher power of the human mind, a power of an onto-logical order higher than any mere brain as such.

For example: imagine two actors on a stage, appar-ently seeing nothing other than themselves, or one an-other, each probably terrified by the economic spectacle within the trans-Atlantic region now, or horrified by a mysteriously queer sound emanating from an intellec-tual darkness by which they are, in effect, overwhelmed.

One of the most useful of such experiences as that, can be presented, with hope of some moderate success, by the proper pedagogical use of the Classical theatrical stage.

There are two principal means for introducing the audience, preferably qualified scientists of the type I might point out to you here, to presentation of an ex-perimental demonstration of the principle of metaphor. There are reasonable alternatives to that approach, but, while defensible approximations, they will fail, none-theless, in any attempt to come directly to the crucial point of scientific principle. I have presented the nature of the basis in truth for the actually needed solution's crafted attempt at alternatives; but, they can not fail to present difficulties for the person lacking the recom-mended grounding in method.

I present my preferred argument as follows.

I. The Physical Science of Mind

In what often passes, unfortunately, for customary doctrine on the subject of the human mind today, the primary emphasis is placed, mistakenly, on the topics of "sense perception" and "the (physical) brain." In modern physical science, the needed healthful change, is away from those popular habits, and must be cen-tered, then, on such sources as the concluding, third section of Bernhard Riemann's habilitation disserta-tion, and such as the successive developments of what have been specifically Lejeune Dirichlet's and Bern-hard Riemann's developments within the category of Abelian Functions. The attempted mathematical reduc-tionist's interpretations of so-called Abelian functions, are to be avoided as being in the likeness of suspected highway-hazards. So, Riemann had forewarned his reader in the concluding sentence of his 1854 habilita-tion dissertation.

The significance of the argument to be made on this account, is that the act of expressing standard human sense-perception, does not show us the actual function of the physical process on which that evidence depends. In effect, the limitations of our sense-perceptual instru-ments are the source of the errors which the careless mind imposes upon what careless opinion lends the false identity of "natural." That fault is inherent in the nature of belief in "sense-perception" as being self-evi-dent (as in the literal meaning of "sense-perception"). Sense-perception does not show us the foot, but only the footprint which the foot has created in its passage. In brief, the "actual foot" is invisible to the sensory ap-paratus; only the virtual shadow (e.g., "the footprint") is visible.

We must proceed from the vantage-point of recog-nizing that what is customarily treated as sense-certain-ties, are, in actual practice, merely shadows cast by what the senses do not present to us directly; there, the existence of true science begins. The habituated belief in a primary value for sense-perception is the most vi-cious systemic folly of the majority of opinion, even among most scientific opinion, still today.

Continue the study of this matter, by extending "the model" of "the foot" to the case in which the "foot" is now extended to the case of a trail of "footprints." The foot itself, including its movements, continues to be ac-tually invisible to the observing person; only the "foot-print" (the shadow of the continuous trail of "foot-prints"), is visible. What, then, is the ontological "place" in which the "foot" itself ("the actual effect") is "visi-ble" in some sense?

Therefore, the actual "foot" in this case, is invisible to the person observing the trail; it is the "virtual shadow" of the series of the merely apparent "foot-events," which is the "visible" expression of the pres-ence of the actual "foot." The real action is thus ex-pressed, only in the form of that which is not seen

The famous prologue to Shakespeare's "Henry V" provides "the touch of counterfeit magic which brings on the awe on which the perceived passion of the induced irony in the drama depends for its equivalent of 'life.'"

THE LIFE OF HENRY V

[I. Prologue]

Enter Chorus

Chorus. O for a Muse of fire, that would ascend
The brightest heaven of invention:
A kingdom for a stage, princes to act,
And monarchs to behold the swelling scene.
Then should the warlike Harry, like himself,
Assume the port of Mars, and at his heels,
Leashed in like hounds, should Famine, Sword, and Fire
Crouch for employment. But pardon, gentles all,
The flat unraiséd spirits that hath dared
On this unworthy scaffold to bring forth   10
So great an object. Can this cockpit hold
The vasty fields of France? or may we cram
Within this wooden O the very casques
That did affright the air at Agincourt?
O, pardon! since a crooked figure may
Attest in little place a million;
And let us, ciphers to this great accompt,
On your imaginary forces work....
Suppose within the girdle of these walls
Are now confined two mighty monarchies,   20
Whose high uprearéd and abutting fronts
The perilous narrow ocean parts asunder.
Piece out our imperfections with your thoughts:
Into a thousand parts divide one man,
And make imaginary puissance.
Think, when we talk of horses, that you see them
Printing their proud hoofs i'th'receiving earth:
For 'tis your thoughts that now must deck our kings,
Carry them here and there: jumping o'er times;
30 Turning th'accomplishment of many years
Into an hour-glass: for the which supply,
Admit me Chorus to this history;
Who prologue-like your humble patience pray,
Gently to hear, kindly to judge, our play.   ['*exit.*'

literally.

So, far, there is nothing which should seem absurd to a competent scientist about any of this. The irony of the imagery lies in the fact that the presumption of "seeing" is not a direct representation, ontologically, of the actual movement of the foot itself; it is the visual experience of the actual movement of the foot, not the foot itself, which has authored the viewer's sense of the perception of both the object and its motion; it is the duty of the scientist to effect the needed correction in what has been accepted scientific opinion. That now poses the question: "What is 'it' which 'sees' that which is embodied in the actuality of observing the multiply paradoxical characteristic of the array of the attributed motion of the designated object as such?"

Now, consider another aspect of that which bears on such kinds of relations. We have thus, now, entered the domain of Shakespeare's and Shelley's ontological paradoxes. Consider a case of the inherent irony of Shakespeare's "Chorus" from *Henry the Fifth*.

What the occasion of a successful stage performance pretends to regard as merely the appearance of the actors, is the fact that the actors standing in for the ghost-like roles of what are actually performed as the work of the actors, have been implicitly assigned to substitute for the image of the characters which they are played to represent, characters from the play itself, which dwell among us, otherwise, only as inhabitants of the audience's imagination.

Meanwhile, as to the drama as a whole, treat it as if you were being advised by the thinking of the voice of a Shakespeare caught in the moment of his writing the famous prologue from his *Henry the Fifth*. On the crucial implications of the subject of that prologue, it is urgent that the following be said here and now.

The characters who appear on the Classical stage of Shakespeare, are made up to appear as virtually ghosts, not the living bodies of the characters being played. The actual ghosts on whose account the actors perform on stage, are to be recognized as actors on stage who are performing the apparent parts of persons which they are actually not; thus, they appear like ghosts attributed to the action of the characters assigned to the drama to perform as ghosts, actual ghosts on stage which the audience chooses to recognize as hypothetically the flesh-and-blood actors, or actor-like objects on stage. However, pay close attention to the fact, that the actors about to appear on the stage are not the real persons (but correspond to a place ostensibly occupied by real persons), while very little of the rest of the impedimenta hauled so onto the stage, is really what it is presumed to represent.

The apparent fault, or, you might say "irony" of the arrangements on stage, is not to be regarded as demanded by the producer's yearning for ready cash, or some other sort of difference expressed as of that category. This feature of the staging of the Classical drama, is an essential part of the meaning of the entirety of the play, a requirement demanded, as a matter of ontological principle, as in the instance of Lady Macbeth's bloody night-prowl, by that principle of metaphor—the principle of the imagination—on which the competence of all dramatic forms of public events depends, as a matter of the principle of true drama. So, Shakespeare's instructions on the crafting of that spectre which is his Birnam Wood, is the necessary touch of gloomy magic without which the grisly irony of an effective conclusion of the drama were not accomplished. All this and its likeness, is the touch of counterfeit magic which brings on the awe on which the perceived passion of the induced irony in the drama depends for its equivalent of "life."

We must induce in the spectators, and also the players, that sense of "magic" on which the competence of the poetry depends. This is not a "trick." At this point, I must introduce one of my specific clarifications:

Hence, we have, there, a proper sort of conventional image of the principle of metaphor as it bursts the bounds of what are merely entertainments, thus to expose itself as the essential principle of a valid physical science, as, unfortunately relatively few presumed scientists have yet actually grasped this notion. The principle of metaphor must be introduced to the action of the drama, at that junction, for such purposes! On this account, the Classical drama, or its like, passes over from entertainment, to the subject of deeply impassioned, seemingly magical principles situated within an enlarged practice of physical science. It proceeds as follows from this point onward.

Make no mistake; this is a matter of real physical science! It is necessary to make the apparent mere play mimic nature, for the sake of the purpose that sense-perception as such can not mimic actual nature; therefore, the poet and dramatist must intimate the magic attributably inherent in history's nature.

Metaphor!

This expression of the principle of metaphor, is the application to a set of functional relationships represented by what are regarded directly as actions in nature for which the action itself is invisible to ordinary sense-perception, but in which for the action itself, even when its nature is physically invisible, we are then potentially enabled to adduce that which remains literally invisible respecting the action recognizable as being of this type of action. This notion tends to be made clear when one assesses the Classical stage from the standpoint of a Platonic physical science in the tradition of such as Heraclitus and Plato, rather than as merely entertainment or the like.

Ordinarily, we "see" what sense-perception presents, not that which the alternate "sensorium" of the domain of physical science proffers as the appropriate alternative.

The most significant expression of this principle of the stage, is located within the actual, but "physically invisible" actions which the successful on-stage performance makes suggestibly "real" for the sake of the audience reactions to what has been passing among the imagination, of the players onstage and the audience alike, or, as a physical interaction which is, in its core, not directly intelligence relevant to the subject of the action itself; here, *the effect of the action*, rather *than a direct vision of the action*, serves as the seemingly "magical" substitute for that occasion. The example of the opening of Chorus from Shakespeare's **King Henry V**, is an excellent illustration of the sense of that which must be the eeriness of the action portrayed to the audience, then and there.

In that part of Shakespeare's drama, pathetic mere toys serve as shadows of that which lacks the mysterious passion of the settings within which the listed characters prance and speak.

On this account, we must recognize a chain of connecting points throughout a real time and conceived place; we must recognize them as points of reference for a universe within which no actual "space" actually exists. It is an experience which should prompt a recollection of the genius of such excellent qualities of ancient anti-reductionists as Heraclitus and Plato, as, also, that of such modern exemplars of the same legacy: exemplars such as the modern European Renaissance's Filippo Brunelleschi, Nicholas of Cusa, and such dependent followers of Cusa as Leonardo da Vinci, Johannes Kepler, Gottfried Leibniz, and soon (speaking historically) after that, such contemporaries and followers of Leibniz as Alexander von Humboldt, Carl F. Gauss, and then Lejeune Dirichlet, Bernhard Riemann, and then such as Max Planck and Albert Einstein. All of these true modern spirits of science, especially since the birth of Europe's Fifteenth Century, had depended chiefly, in their respective lifetimes, on the systemically defined heritage of the crucial, ontological implications of Cusa's *De Docta Ignorantia* (*On Learned Ignorance.*)

Then, there is the matter of that which needs to be postponed for a moment here, postponed for consideration as being probably both an intrinsically elementary point, and also one yet to be presented, until now; I present this, for the purpose of situating what I must present as the relevant, still higher standpoint of argument needed to make clear the crucially important, and presently still little-known Classical principle which I am emphasizing here.

Philo vs. Euclid & Nietzsche

To put that just-stated point here: that which is to be put aside so for the present moment, we have the case of the popular, but typically, systemically absurd notion of the modern reductionist's echo of the fraudulent presumptions of Euclid. On this account, see Philo of Alexandria's denunciation of Euclid, and, (implicitly) of Euclid's modern, fascist follower, Friedrich Nietzsche: all of which is implicitly generic in its implications.

The deeper aspect of that same issue of Philo versus Euclid (and Aristotle) touches the ontologically crucial implications of the notion of continuing, universal creativity, as that which interpenetrates the actual reality necessarily, underlying the principle of the notion of universe itself.

That much said this far, to get to the core of the point to be made in this presentation, we must now proceed as follows into the matter of "The Science of Classical Art."

The notion that sense-perceptions are real, as if in and of themselves, is among the more deadly of the common, and often poisonous, superstitions to be met among the credulously symbol-minded. Indeed, the most tragic follies of most of past and present mankind, can be blamed on this.

Those may not seem to be the worst nightmares of ordinary mankind; but, the belief in a self-evident quality for sense-perception for itself, is the source of what have been the worst, most systematically vicious ef-

"The belief in a self-evident quality for sense-perception for itself, is the source of what have been the worst, most systematically vicious effects upon the mind of mankind." Here, the disciple Thomas does not believe that Jesus has been resurrected, until his senses have been convinced. Rembrandt's "Doubting Thomas" (1634).

fects upon the mind of mankind. Those so-duped believers, have swallowed the foolish, and implicitly poisonous notion, that the sense-perceptions are not only reality, but are even to be considered as the foundations in evidence for an experienced truth. In fact, what those images actually represent, are only the twisted, often unreal shadows, which have been cast by unknown objects. These are objects which may exist for some audiences as if they had been sent from another universe, rather than the one which actually exists; these are the mere shadows which most among us in the society, thus far, each tends to mistake for having been their own true being.

The customary notion of sense-perception, is sane only insofar as the believer claims a sense-perception to be no more than merely the evidence of the occurrence of that which has the effect of what is attributed as having been a sense-perception, but not a reality in and of itself. It is to be considered as if it were no more truthful than being merely a footprint left by the passage of an invisible foot.

The principle to which I have pointed in the immediately preceding two paragraphs here, is often already available in a relatively perfected, truthful form, in great Classical artistic compositions. The principle of truth, so expressed, is properly identified as the great, all-revolutionary principle of metaphor, upon which all true knowledge, like all truly Classical artistry, depends.

The distinction of the principle of metaphor, is that the actual relationships among the direct objects of the metaphor are not directly inter active; they are images which might merely glare, or smile at one another, each within the silenced confinement of its own glass cage, but they can not interact willfully. Only the passions within and among those such qualities of certain objects of our imagination, are, as if seen in a glass cage, or, as one playwright has said, "a glass menagerie," what taunts the imageries, as the Christian Apostle Paul wrote of this matter in *I Corinthians* 13:

> *"For now, we see through a glass, darkly; but, then, face to face; now, I know in part; but, then, shall I know, even as I am known."*

This passage from the Apostle Paul has a precise, scientific meaning in the realities of physical time, as I emphasized in such locations as my relatively brief, September 30, 2011 replies to two questions presented to me in a LaRouche PAC national webcast on that occasion. I explain this crucial fact of a competent physical science, as follows, at a place somewhat later in this report, below.

So, it is the expression of the true principle of metaphor, that we must, typically, consider two objects, each of which is not a reality in itself, but each of which is, rather, a seen shadow cast by an unseen reality. What, therefore, is the relationship of that which is seen, as if in a mirror, as an imagined relationship between what appear to be two different objects? The objects which we have believed that we have seen, must be treated as related in the way that the mere shadows of real objects must be related to the human actor. They are related in metaphor.

That, for example, was precisely the true nature of the stroke of genius in Johannes Kepler's recognition of his discovered principle of universal gravitation, as in, also, his relevant, earlier discovery of the use of the notion of a "vicarious hypothesis." Such is the actual relationship between the shadows known as sense-perceptions, and the unseen objective-existences which are invisible to human sense-perceptions; such is the quandary of those persons, who differ from, but resemble, curiously, the behavior of those apparently panicked pigs which react to the earthquakes at a discrete interval of time prior to a human perception of such an actually, humanly experienced, subsequent event.

Pierre-Simon Laplace's Demon

So, Pierre-Simon Laplace lacked the honesty of the pigs experiencing the onset of that which we humans have experienced as the pigs' own first, direct perception of the earthquake as being a sensed earthquake. Such is the conclusion to be adduced in noting the intrinsic incompetence of Laplace's fraudulent report on the actuality which is usually mistaken for what was merely an imagined form of space-time.

The recent half-billion years of the related, known physical-scientific history of life under the hosting of our galaxy, demonstrates that what might seem to some, to be the likeness of a "self-evident clock time" does not actually exist as anything more than the effect of the shadows which had been mistaken for the adumbrated notion of the actual event. The real "clock" of this universe, acts through physical-evolutionary time, the time of ontological revolutions among sundry varieties of species, not "pill-like" doses of objects in clock-time. There is no constantly fixed time in an actual physical space-time; time is what you become in this universe while you have lived, and remain living, and, also continue to have been. I shall proffer a clearer view of this particular fact under the heading of the principle of creativity to which I responded in those closing moments of my September 30, 2011 national webcast.

Having taken that much into account for later reference here, I now say on that account, in brief, that the notion of a "Second Law of Thermodynamics" which was cooked up by Nineteenth-century hoaxsters such as Rudolf Clausius, is an assertion directly contrary to the most essential scientific facts respecting development and extinctions in the course of the efficiently evolutionary development of the known universe, respecting our present knowledge of the evolution of life-forms during the recent half-billion years. Evolution of life forms, in particular, is to be measured in terms of a required pattern of increase of the rates of energy-flux density of the experienced universe, as in such cases as the continuing existence of life-forms' determining power to increase the required such relative increase of density. The successful existence of living species, moves as if with joyful passion against what must seem to the mechanist as a virtually uphill gradient of our universe. Our universe proceeds successfully, and, I wish to believe it should be happily, in the experience of its successive economic-uphill transformations.[1]

In particular, during the recent half-billion years of the relevant evidence, the clock of the evolution of species on this planet, proceeds uphill. "Clock time" does not exist as an independent factor of physical time; physical time exists as an "uphill" development; it moves "uphill," as from lower to higher, qualitative expressions of existence, such as higher "energy-flux density" of existence. Stagnation, otherwise known as "zero growth," or, as the illusion of belief in "clock time," is a measure of attrition, a measure of degradation and, ultimately, "extinction" of that whose breeding had failed. In the real universe, existence demands the opportunity to move as if "up-hill," and, for many, seemingly against the grain; all of this, seemingly, to the effect of a principle of universal anti-entropy; therefore, a trend of extinction is inherent in the cases of a lack of what seems to be uphill progress toward higher mean states of existence.

The Oligarchical Lie

Those facts present us with a twofold challenge.

First, since the fact of the conclusive weight of experimental evidence, is that the pretended discovery of the notion of a mean rate of "zero-growth," is inherently a lie; therefore, the consequent question is, whence came the fraudulent notion of "zero growth"—the so-called "Second Law of Thermodynamics"?

The answer to that question is relatively simple; the answer, which is to say, the name of the culprit, is the brutish (e.g., "British") fraud called "the oligarchical principle." The second challenge is: "Who is setting that oligarchical clock?" My suggested answer is, as the Apostle Peter's associate, Philo of Alexandria, pointed out: there is an inherent, upward trajectory of continu-

ing development in the "physics" of our universe: hence, the inherent need to combat the evil by the use of such means as those which are typified by the physics-concept of a universal, anti-entropic, anti-Euclidean, anti-Friedrich Nietzschean rejection of Euclid's assertion of the notion of a "dead Creator" in a universe in which there is no inherently continuing creation permitted according to Aristotle and Euclid and their asserted "universal laws."

The belief in a so-called "Second Law of Thermodynamics" is an expression of the moral as much as the physical decadence which inheres in, and is characteristic of the practice of the so-called "oligarchical principle."

That "oligarchical principle" of the current British Royal household and its impedimenta, is what is illustrated by the principle of the first of the four stages (thus far) of the Roman Empire; the second, had been passage of that empire into its reincarnation as Byzantium; thence, third, into the Venetian-directed status of the Crusader pandemic; and, fourthly, the latter's re-emergence as the present British empire under the descendants of the Sarpian, imperial New Venetian Party's William of Orange. It had emerged, then, as the present British empire, that of, now, the Queen Elizabeth II currently seeking its realization in the form of something akin to the notion of a frankly pro-satanic, thermonuclear Armageddon expressed as the intention to effect the rapid, genocidal reduction of the present human species, from seven billions, now, to one billion living persons permitted to exist on Earth, by order of the Queen's own realm. In its earlier incarnations, this same oligarchical tradition had included such atrocities as the trend into decadence of what had been the relatively superior quality of the Indian Ocean-based maritime culture of the Sumerians, as by the moral decline effected through the effects of the disastrous Peloponnesian War.

There are deeper considerations beyond those indicated here this far; the following issues are of crucial significance on that account.

Mankind in the Universe

Consider the inherently anti-entropic direction which the evidence of science to date has shown during the extent of the course of about a half-billion years' pageant of what is presently known as the estimated

---

1. This is the subject featured in the question and answer portion of my national webcast address of September 30, 2011.

half-billion years of the succession of known life-forms on Earth. Review that evidence, when such a sequence of developments has been matched with the trends in that galaxy within which our Solar system is contained, and that tallied when the evidence of the noëtic principle of universal creativity has been exhibited in the emergence and continuing development of our Sun's planetary system.

However, there is another, considerably deeper phase of this matter, which is to be considered here now. Although I have presented much of this which I state here, which had already been emphasized in my earlier publications, there are strong reasons for my restating this absolutely crucial case to this present audience, here and now.

The principal, persisting source of incompetence among even many presumably ranking scientists, has been the fruit of the grave error of a continuing insistence on what are regarded as merely sense-perceptions, which are now often misused as a claimed standard of scientific certainties. The essential fact to be considered in this respect, is that sense-perceptions are exactly that: merely sense-perceptions, and, relative to the successes of the Riemann standard in physics, childishly crude instruments. Those sense-perceptions are experiences which have the actual relevance of being merely sense-perceptions, and which are often expressions of some misleading qualities associated with mere shadows of actuality, rather than being, actually, a not-directly-sense-experienced bit of evidence which could be better represented, directly, as the probably actually generated laws of the universe itself.

Consider some timely thoughts.

The principle underlying the point which I have just outlined here, could be conveniently described, in effect, as a matter of a distinction of, most notably, two ontologically different conceptions of the experience of what is perceived as having been "physical time." The simplest view of the kinds of distinctions to be considered along the lines I have outlined in these preceding paragraphs, is the suggestion of the difference between the shadow (human sense-perception and its specific effects, on the one side) and the actual experience of the

> **The principal, persisting source of incompetence among even many presumably ranking scientists, has been the fruit of the grave error of a continuing insistence on what are regarded as merely sense-perceptions, which are now often misused as a claimed standard of scientific certainties.**

universality of the real event, on the other.

Let us illustrate the working point here by aid of devices which, on the one side, are the relatively causal factor of the precursor of an earthquake, and on the other, the perceived effect of what was the "originally radiated" effect later experienced as the human experience of the earthquake itself. All human sense-perceptions which duped people attribute to be the virtually self-evident authority of "sense-certainty," are effects of the latter type which I have just outlined here. Such is the difference between the human sensorium's attribution of "felt developments" by human sense-perception, and the more accurate, and also more timely radiation of that which has been responsible for the delayed impact expressed as what should be reported as human sensory or comparable experience.

So, on the one side, we have the crude instruments known as living, biological sense-perceptions; on the other side we have the crafted precision of physical instruments which reach toward both the infinitely large and infinitesimally small, as Bernhard Riemann warned us of this fact.

Our sense perceptions are a crude attempt at simulation of what is experienced more closely to the actual event felt, perhaps, a bit later and in a differing modality.

Thus, in this same fashion, the most useful of the early known cases of actually physical-scientific evidence, rather than merely sense-perceptual beliefs, are to be met in such cases as the duplication of the cube by the associate of Plato known as the Pythagorean Archytas, as the latter's celebrated, systemically crucial discovery of the duplication of the cube, complements the statement in the celebrated fragment of Heraclitus, and kindred accomplishments from ancient times.

This discrepancy in "time" of occurrence, to which I have referred immediately above, that as in respect to human sense-perception as such, is thus to be appreciated as a systemic defect in any human reliance on a presumed "natural" quality of what we recognize in the use of the technical term "sense-perception." A similar conclusion is needed when the sense-perception of the

"On the one side, we have the crude instruments known as living, biological sense-perceptions; on the other side, we have the crafted precision of physical instruments which reach toward both the infinitely large and infinitesimally small. . . ." Shown: Goddard's Earth Resources Technology Satellite, launched in 1982.

pigs experiencing an earthquake-related type of event, is contrasted with the same real event's later report of a human response to the same setting of the in-process-ness experienced by the pigs of the categorically "same" event.

The essential challenge which my cited treatment of the difference between the pigs and the people during the same extended world event, illustrates more broadly, is what is rooted in the inherent imperfections of what can be reduced, by aid of man-made scientific instruments, to a common universal event. The mistaken notion of an alleged human experience of "space-time," is an illustration of such inherent errors in the various species of notions of lapsed time associated within a generality of notions equivalent to those of sense-perception.

It could, and should be proposed that no man sees the universe as the Creator does. The warning which this represents, is that sense-perception does not produce what is fairly and truly regarded as an actually scientific certainty. We must train the modern human mind to rely on a vast, and broadly extended proliferation of conflicting perceptors, so that we might, in this way, provide ourselves with a vast array of instruments em-

ployed to supersede the crude mechanisms of what we are customarily duped into regarding as "direct evidence." As we are now forewarned, more and more, of the deadly menace of being drawn into a misguided faith in ordinary "sense-perception," we are being presently warned, that we require a vast, and vastly expanding array of instruments, out of which, following the noble and unique achievement of Kepler's discovery of gravitation, we must build up a vastly enriched kind of sensorium, by means of which we are enabled to free our human species from the folly of faith in merely ordinary human sense-perceptions.

This brings us to the matter of the foolishness of Pierre-Simon Laplace.

Among what should be regarded as the most notable failures of persons such as that Laplace, is the use of the notion of "clock-time," or an equivalent, as the adopted primary means for measuring the behavior of the universe as if "from the outside." A few crucial remarks on this will be sufficient at this immediate juncture.

"What is the clock which measures the time of the clock?" To translate that into the complementary argument: "How much of the total time of action is absorbed by variations in the rate of variation in what is merely presumed to be a constant rate of clock-time?" There is nothing idle, as a matter of principle, in that question. The clock-time of the lapsed terms of about a half-billion years of life which has been "clocked" in our galaxy, is one neat little hoax of the accomplices of the fraud of the "Second Law of Thermodynamics."

Rudolf Clausius' hoax of "A Second Law," runs "smack" against two notable obstacles. First, the idea of a fixed galactic time, is defined by his argument as external to the action within the universe; second, that the expression of an overall actual rate expressed in the system of clock-time, is the somewhat embarrassing effect of the expression of relative gain in the higher forms of life within the system during the course of the recent half-billion years.

That, and related considerations show Clausius to be some sort of outright hoaxster.[2] The error becomes

____

2. Cf. Turn to page 293 of the Heinrich Weber edition of ***Bernhard Riemann's Gesammelte Mathematische Werke***. B.G. Teubner, Stuttgart, 1892/1902, p. 293, footnote by editor: Heinrich Weber's hoax pub-

"The first available body of systemically crucial evidence bearing on the required principles of modern physical science, was actually presented by Cardinal Nicholas of Cusa, in his De Docta Ignorantia." Shown: Wall tomb of Cusa (d. 1464), San Pietro in Vincoli, Rome; Andrea Bregno. Cusa in prayer, left; St. Peter enthroned, center; Angel of the Resurrection, on the right.

more interesting when we take into account that living processes are increasing the relative anti-entropy of their category, and that the relative anti-entropy expressed by a science-driven human culture, is a higher rate of anti-entropy than merely living creatures. Then, there is the matter of the relative rates of anti-entropy among the categories of merely animal life. "Who measured, or actually crafted, your fraudulently crafted, oligarchical yardstick, Herr Clausius?"

The ability of the human species to maintain and increase the energy-flux-density factor of society, that in inverse proportion to the oligarchical factor, attests to the fact that there is nothing natural about the pack of lies called "environmentalism." The issue is the degenerative effect of oligarchist social systems, such as the British monarchy, a mass-murderous effect which is inherent in the current British oligarchical "agenda."[3]

If I seem to speak meanly of the alleged co-thinkers of Herr Clausius, Queen Elizabeth II, and her lackey John Schellnhuber, their claims are not a product of science, but of the psychological needs of an oligarchical system associated with the myth of the Olympian Zeus, and, probably, sometimes, some cult of cannibalism.

To deal further with the phenomenon of oligarchism, we must turn our attention to the intertwined principles of progress and the practice of advances in physical science. The case of Cardinal Nicholas of Cusa and his hereditary influence on the shaping of scientific and social progress of mankind, provides us with the cornerstone of the matters which we must take up next.

lished on behalf of a fraud concocted by the mathematician Rupert Clausius.

3. As the point is referenced elsewhere within this report, the origin of Rupert Clausius' hoax is traced to the a-priorist tradition of the reductionism of such hoaxsters as the poisoner Aristotle and of Euclid. That reductionist school is rooted in the oligarchist system associated with the morally corrupt, mathematics tradition of such as the Olympian Zeus, for which money is a God of the principle of imperialism, such as the successive incarnations of the Roman imperial tradition. Money, like an a-priorist system of number-worship, is defined as a god above gods, as "outside," as a-priori above all actual knowledge of the system of physical existence of the human species and its scientific practice (e.g., ancient and contemporary monetarism). This monetarist dogma is the continuing foundation of all imperialist and related practices. Indeed, all true Marxists are intrinsically imperialists (monetarists: "money worshippers") in the Roman imperial and related traditions.

Cusa's Modern European Epoch

Whereas, in modern European science, there are potent and true contributions by Filippo Brunelleschi; the first available body of systemically crucial evidence bearing on the required principles of modern physical science, was actually presented by Cardinal Nicholas of Cusa, in his ***De Docta Ignorantia***. All modern notions of scientific principle contrary to Cusa on this account, have been the product of regressions to the debased notions of the oligarchical principle.

All of the leading competent human personalities of modern science, through the production of Johannes Kepler's works, were explicitly followers of Cusa; the leading scientist to emerge as a follower of Cusa student Kepler, was the Gottfried Leibniz who created the modern calculus premised on a discovery of a physical principle by the same Gottfried Leibniz. All of the key-stone progress of modern physical science and Classical artistic cultures, is premised on the same consideration, as the case of Johann Sebastian Bach demonstrates. Leibniz, in turn, was, thus, a cardinal figure echoed in the Nineteenth-century founding of the physical science of the school of such followers of Abraham Kästner and Carl F. Gauss as Alexander v. Humboldt's Lejeune Dirichlet, Bernhard Riemann, and of the continuing achievements of followers from among such leading figures of Twentieth-century science as Max Planck and Albert Einstein.

Such is the outline of the hopes and also the contrary, wildly reductionist, even systemically criminal abominations perpetrated within the bounds of modern physical science since the founding of that science, by Nicholas of Cusa, which had broken European civilization free of the Fourteenth-century "New Dark Age." This has been a breakthrough centered in that initiating role for all modern science which had been launched by such as Brunelleschi and Nicholas of Cusa. Excepting extraordinary cases such as the economic and related reforms under Charlemagne, virtually all European civilization, to the present day, expresses an imperialist (i.e., monetarist) system of society, as typified in effects by the four principal manifestations of the Roman Empire, from the original Roman Empire of Caesar Augustus through the British empire of Queen Elizabeth II today. The notion of the role of money per se as the monetarist principle of four successive expressions of what had been the original Roman Empire, outlines the relationship between monetarism and imperialism in the world today. The present breakdown-crisis of the trans-Atlantic monetarist system, is a typical expression of the causes of the onrushing doom within the presently crashing, British-dominated, trans-Atlantic monetarist-imperialist pestilence.

These bare outlines of what is customarily presented as the outline of the ancient through modern history of European-centered accounts of culture, could not be competently presented today, without great emphasis on the wicked role in which the effect of a moral disease called "the oligarchical tradition" is taken into account for its role as a customary, damning feature of that span of European-centered history.

This has been experienced as oligarchical self-damnations such as the ancient Peloponnesian War, or of the Satanic hues of ancient Babylon, or of the wicked effects of the poisoning of Alexander the Great at the prompting of Aristotle, and, also, the successive waves of a recurring Roman Empire of, first, Rome, then Byzantium, and then the Venetian rule over the pestilence of the so-called "crusaders," and, presently, the New Venetian Party of William of Orange, which paved the way for the British version of the Roman imperial system of today. All these have tended to prevent any ostensibly competent modern historian from bringing forth even a single principle of the culture of ancient through modern European civilization.

Such attempts at civilization as those, have each been not as much a culture, as much as it has been a reflection of a recurring, see-saw battle for the reign of an evil which is contrary to the intended true nature of our human species. All this has been contrary to a continuing battle for the good, a battle which has resisted, but not always successfully, the tyrannies typified by the specific oligarchical evil of the model of the British imperial monarchy of today.

So, the genius of Cardinal Nicholas of Cusa, who inspired the trans-oceanic emergence of what would be included as the becoming of our United States in North America, typifies the unique achievement of the creation of our own United States of America, but, on the other side of history, there has been the recurring evil which has often ruined our wonderful republic through the continuing existence of the Romantic evil known as the British empire. Cusa's ***De Docta Ignorantia*** remains today the model for trans-Atlantic designs of anti-imperialist, anti-monetarist systems spread throughout the world at large.

There should be nothing considered as an inevitably evil outcome in the record of evil marked out by the recurring moral failures of the Mediterranean region in particular. It has been a moral sickness, a pestilence rightly identified as "oligarchism," which has been chiefly responsible for the evil effects in European cultures so far. What has cursed the nations of Europe during most of their periods of existence thus far, has been a single principle of corruption, the corruption best identified as "the oligarchical principle" which has been typified by such manifestations as the Peloponnesian War, as the great dramatic historian Aeschylus has exhibited the relevant evidence on that tragedy and its outcome.

Is "Oligarchism" "Satan Worship?"

Whatever a person's choice of a religious prejudice might be, the singular fact of the span of history of the Mediterranean region, from the earliest known political history, to the present time, has been what is sometimes regarded as the revolt of Christianity against the frankly Satanic quality of the four stages of the Roman empires, including today's British empire, and their legacies. That cumulative legacy of the four phases of what had been the original Roman Empire, has been the authentically Satanic tradition presently embedded as a certain system of law embedded in the British branch of that presently four-fold Empire, still today.

The British empire emerged to life from its original kernel, as the traditions of England's Henry VIII and, a bit later, of William of Orange's Sarpian "New Venetian" party. William's nominally Dutch,"New Venetian Party" of the followers of Paolo Sarpi, persists, to this present day, as the immediate origin of the evil which is presently, deeply embedded in the British empire of Queen Elizabeth II, as in that of her horrid spouse, and in the images of the sucking vampire bats which the royal pair appears to love so tenderly: as it has been said, each night.

This statement, just made by me here, is not a fancied spawn of any mere prejudice. As I shall emphasize, without toleration of compromise here, that which I have reported here thus far, is a physical-scientific fact, one which must be considered as such in defining that intention, an opinion contrary to the inherently evil spirit of the British empire, an opinion which is affirmed in the true nobility of the natural inclination of our human species.

Such, is the setting of the oligarchical principle. Such is the crafting of the oligarchical tradition which the legacy of the Roman empire expresses so aptly. Such is the evil from which we must free mankind now, if the presently looming risk of a global thermonuclear holocaust, is to be avoided during the immediate period ahead. We must, of course, resist that danger; but, we must do better than merely resist; we must dig out the source of this presently immediate menace, and uproot it. Therefore, I must now describe and define what we must uproot and destroy.

The Human Mind: Again, in Principle

An important thought in transition.

The customary view of the function of the human mind is, unfortunately, still rooted in the errant, naive presumptions of sense-perception. The fault embedded in notions of "sense certainty," is what should be recognized as the obvious fact that sense-perceptions, whether considered in part, or as a collection of the sensory functions of our bodily incarnation, are not the lawful expression of that universe which credulously mistaken persons presume to be their experience of truth.

For this case, truth is to be extended to include all of the direct and indirect experiences of both mind and body combined. All of the factors of that experience which affect the human species, directly or indirectly, in the individual, or in the experience of mankind on Earth as a whole, are experiences which must be taken into account for the purpose of forming a judgment on the actual totality of what the human mind should be taking into account for any specific, systematic kind of decision.

What "I experience," or what I might have picked up from neighborly or other "outside" sources, has the predominant tendency to distract our processes of judgment away from truth, toward the lies of dream-lands' fantasies. As the case of the best practice of modern physical science illustrates the point, actual truth in shaping opinions depends, properly, on judging that which simple sense-perception, whether sensed, or borrowed, inherently misjudges.

Science? What Is Truth?

Now, when I have said as much as I think necessary to be said on the subjects of what I have presented, or prominently referenced otherwise, thus far, I bring what has been the lurking core-subject of this report, to the fore.

As the exemplary physicist Bernhard Riemann emphasized in the concluding sentence of his 1854 habilitation dissertation: What, we must ask ourselves, is that which is pathologically wrong about the manner of the teaching of mathematics as such, in schools still today? What are the implications of that systematic error of the mathematicians for the crisis of economy today? Why did Riemann emphasize the urgency of departing from the department of mathematics, for the sake of an actually physical science, thus displacing a depraved practice in the tradition of a Euclid?

Return our attention, again, to the illustrative, tragic case of the pathetic Pierre-Simon Laplace.

Refer, again, to the case of that utter fraud known as Euclidean geometry, as a leading case in point. Or, take the fact that, despite every so-called principle of science claimed for Sir Isaac Newton, the Newtonian doctrine, like that of Euclid, has been shown, sweepingly, to have been a systemic fraud; the same is to be said of the doctrine of Aristotle and, as Philo of Alexandria denounced both Aristotle, and also, implicitly, Aristotle's Euclid-like mimic, Friedrich "God is dead!" Nietzsche.

As with the case of Euclid's a-prioristic presumptions, all so-called "scientific" dogma presented as if a-priori, is implicitly a hoax, whether or not the hoaxster is aware of such implicitly intentional implications. However, for this present occasion, rather than focussing our attention on the relatively trivial quality of the fraud permeating Euclid's fundamental, a-priori assumptions, I deal here with the far deeper implications of another, truly vicious fraud: the belief in the implied "self-evidence" of what is identified as the a-priorist's belief in that "a-priori" notion of "time" adopted by the hoaxster Pierre-Simon Laplace. Laplace's fraud, is of crucial importance as a symptom of crucial issues to be brought to a mercilessly compe-

Wikimedia Commons

The great lie of Pierre-Simon Laplace: His "insistence on degrading the universe to the arbitrary presumption of 'clock time.'..."

tent scientific understanding in these matters presented here.[4]

That means, or should be understood to mean, for example, that true science requires that, absolutely contrary to the fraud known as Euclidean geometry, no "external presumptions of so-called principle" should be required, or permitted, to define the subject-matter of the system of human existence itself. This will continue to require special attention from me personally, as from certain others; almost none of our people, excepting some in the "Basement" operations, have an adequate sense of competent insight into the actual implications of what I have just written here. Fortunately, some discussions along those lines have been presented to the "Basement" crew at this time. The problem here, on this account, is that only some among our "Basement" science-crew have presently shown any competent insight into what this matter implies.

The problem even within the leadership and ranks of our own association, is the utter lack of willingness, among not only some, but many professed scientists, to accept the very notion of the possible existence of a grounding in the crucial principles which this matter of physical science involves. Here, the very notion of a standard mathematics predicated on a mathematical form of presumptions, breaks down.

I explain that crucial point, as follows. This is the most deserving choice of "whipping boy" which deserves to be punished for an excellent moral purpose: no expression of that sickly notion of a mathematical form of proof of principle should be practiced; no such notion as that could be regarded as "competent." Only the notion of the existence of the creative powers of the human mind as such, can be used legitimately; no deductive form of argument could be competent

---

4. See the opening two paragraphs of Bernhard Riemann's habilitation dissertation, where the relevant, pathological history of mathematics is summarized, as also, of course, in the closing sentence of that dissertation.

The oligarchical system: "The most often recognized characteristic of the evil which is the present British Empire, lies in the central significance of its monetarist system." Shown: The British Royal Family.

for addressing the fundamental issues invoked. Only a type of formulation associated with Max Planck collaborator Wolfgang Köhler's "Gestalt" psychology, and its correlative in the notions of "mental health" associated with certain minority strains of psychoanalysis, provide a describably typical clue to the practical meaning of the argument which I have just invoked.

To provide a decent approximate image of what those remarks of mine actually signify, imagine a being whose entire world-outlook is that of a creature committed to a self-induced state of its inherent mental health. Think of "a healthy mind" which has no criteria other than an actual coherence based solely on a mentally healthful promotion of the qualitative self-development of itself. The principle to be considered on this account, is that creation of a universe can not be premised on anything external to that universality.

If we attempt to represent such a scheme of things in a deductive mode, nothing works as might be literally prescribed in any conventional sort of way. The effort goes better if we rely on the argument which I introduced in reply to questions, respecting the core-principle of human creativity, which were posed during the concluding moments of my National Broadcast of this past September 30th.

To restate that argument in a necessary way, let it be restated as follows.

The Great Lie of Pierre Laplace[5]

The most crucial of the issues raised during the Nineteenth Century concerning the alleged principles of physical science, has probably been the great lie of Pierre-Simon Laplace: Laplace's insistence on degrading the universe to the arbitrary presumption of "clock time" is of particular notability. The most adequate treatment of Laplace's hoax, so far, has been provided, albeit in a somewhat sketch-like fashion, until now, in my replies to questions respecting time, during the national webcast of September 30, 2011. I shall now pick up the issue of Laplace from where I had referenced it earlier in this report. I shall deal with deeper implications of this in a pre-envisaged piece to be written and published at a coming time.

There are, to begin, actually two intimately related errors in Laplace's celebrated swindle. One is the bald nonsense of Laplace's treatment of the subject of "time" as such; however, that nonsense is implicitly inseparable from a second consideration, the reductionist's presentation of the topic of "energy." In my replies to two of the three questions presented to me in the concluding portion of the national webcast of Sept. 30th, I introduced the "factor" of the application of applied power over intervals of what we call "time." At first blush, my

---

5. At this point, refer extensively to my Chapter II. "The Human Credit System" in **Dumb Democrats!: Principle or Party** (*EIR*, Nov. 11, 2011; LaRouche PAC at http://archive.larouchepac.com/node/20133).

objection might appear to be merely a blush; on closer inspection, it is a torrent which overturns everything for which Laplace's principal utterances have stood. It is the consequent scientific principle which I have relegated to an early production.

Three immediate considerations are the most significant on these accounts this far:

1. That, explicitly contrary to taught popular dogma, is the actually required standard for life in presently known aspects of the galaxy which we inhabit. The fraud to be located at this point is the utterly fraudulent doctrine of a so-called "Second Law of Thermodynamics." The required level of energy-flux density for maintaining life-forms on our planet, has continued to rise in a fashion which threatens to deliver a timely doom for all species which can not muster the means to overcome the effects of a required increase of the mean energy-flux density in the system as a whole.
2. Consequently, the actual "cost" of even the simple maintenance of the system, requires an increase of energy-flux density operating within the system, a fact which proves the fraudulent character, as much as the sheer absurdity of the so-called "Second Law of Thermodynamics."
3. In addition to that set of considerations, a general increase of the "energy-flux density" of the system is required merely to maintain the system at an effective level of "status quo ante." We are currently entering a part of our galaxy for which the indicated existential rule is "grow or die."

There are several prime types of considerations to be brought into play on account of these stated and related considerations. However, the truly crucial problem which is to be recognized in this set of connections, is to be located, essentially, in the effects of the fact that our planet's human system in the large, is still structured, currently, according to the adopted standards which are rooted ("habituated," "conditioned") in that so-called oligarchical system, a system which has unnecessarily dominated society generally during the period of an oligarchical history of known, reigning, organized societies.

The implication is, that even to "stand still" in effect, insofar as known organized society is relevant, an effective increase of the "energy-flux density" of the relevant social systems of organized mankind, requires a rising flow of "energy-flux density" through that society.

The root of the problem which the described case presents to us, is a fact which is expressed otherwise by the simple fact that a required increase of energy-flux density, is needed even to, in effect, "stand still."

That problem, so described, is inherent in the prevalence of the oligarchical model, rather than our habitation of a planetary system as such. The following discussion is more or less indispensable on that account.

If we eliminate oligarchical controls such as those typical of the four successive Roman empires, the inherent evil of the current British empire included, we can show, as a study of the fluctuations in the economic history of the span from the founding and stable existence of the Plymouth settlement and the pre-William of Orange Massachusetts Bay settlement shows, and as the case of the United States and its patterns of rise and decline illustrates the point most dramatically, that, as the normal state of a settled condition of organized society illustrates this, that there is a natural trend toward increase of the effective equivalent of required and actual, relative energy-flux density per capita, in any society which is not suffering effects of an imposed oligarchical system. In other words: eliminate the British empire and its oligarchical likeness throughout the known history of this planet, and there were, then, an available, dominant tendency for an increase of the realized energy-flux density, as may be expressed per capita and per square kilometer of land-area.

Who Is Your Choice of God?

Creativity, as physical science might competently define a notion of a self-subsisting principle of creativity, and science can not be competently distinguished from an expression of perfect self-development. Nothing external to that notion of self-development can be permitted to be taken into consideration as a scientific practice. Everything which exists within those systemic bounds, does not have a freely willfully functional existence "outside" such bounds. What unfolds, hopefully, as a result, is a systemic quality of self-development.

It were not necessary for us to know, beforehand, the pathway of self-development which defines the "rules of behavior" of that self-creative process of self-extension. This self-development assumes the attributable form of an unfolding self-creation. It is neither necessary, nor proper for us to prejudge the rules which govern such a process of self-development of that universe. Rather, we must discover the rules of self-development from a critical examination of the process's own behavior, as the actual Socratic methods demonstrate such effects.

Indeed, once we have required the "explanation" of an "outside factor," we have violated the principle of a process of creation.

The coherence which we might properly recognize in such a process of self-creation, is the equivalent of the morality of the process in "its self-entirety." It is the unfolding coherence of the process which rules over the process, allowing, even demanding what must be done, and what not. It is such coherence within the continually unified process, which defines the system, as within that process of the continuing self-development of the system.

There is one comment to be added to all this. Let us consider the ostensibly "self-correcting" feature of the system as a whole, from the standpoint of what we might prudently term the "sanity" of the system itself. That notion, respecting the notion of a self-perfecting system of the prescribed features, points to an implicit principle of self-conception within the system, an implication which were to be considered as a creative conscience's expression of a state of its "sanity."

However, in all that I have said under those terms, the factor of what is ostensibly a supreme feature of "conscience" must be dominant. This factor can not be "instantaneous," but must be "active," as the sanity of the system considered as a whole must be.

Now, since we have just considered some obvious principles of any notion of a self-universal creation as "the required self-conscience of the system," we must now proceed accordingly. This time, our concern must be to define the practical meaning of that principle of "conscience" which is the active principle of the system: the internal "sanity" of the system as a process.

From Vernadsky's View

That much said here on that account thus far, consider some fairly well-defined, "as necessarily internal," characteristics of that system. The interrelationships among such known "factors" as Academician V.I. Vernadsky's "hierarchical" distinctions of "lithosphere," "biosphere," and "noösphere," are to be considered as useful mooring-points for such a discussion.

From the standpoint of the principally known works of Academician V.I. Vernadsky, as from the mid-1930s onward, Vernadsky's notable principles have depended increasingly upon the standpoint of the Bernhard Riemann who represents the most crucial principles of a physical science incorporating such among his great successors as Max Planck, Albert Einstein, and V.I. Vernadsky himself. No compartmentalization among them can be justly tolerated; the functional interdependence among them, although yet to become fully understood, is monumental.

However, looking backwards to the middle of the Fifteenth Century, the intimations of the work of Filippo Brunelleschi as subsequently overwhelmed by the genius of Nicholas of Cusa expressed in Cusa's ***De Docta Ignorantia***, have no equal in their defining an entirely fresh, ontological notion of physical science for the entire sweep from the century of Cusa. This has been a notion which dominates the foundations of science from that time to the present date. That work, and its companions from the work of that same author, has had the practical effect of bringing to the fore an entirely fresh conception of the role of mankind and science, that from nearly the onset of that century and, hence the A.D. 1401 birth of Cusa himself.

Indeed the very existence of the United States has been a consequence of an injunction of a policy by Cusa: a directive to cross the great oceans, to create new nations to escape the degeneration which the resurgence of the Venetian system of usury had brought down destructively upon the momentary achievements of the Great Ecumenical Council of Florence (1438-1439), the Council in which all of the timely greatness of European culture was then expressed.

The process of social evolution for the good, as expressed by the role of Cusa and his associates in that great Council and its scientific expressions, was at the root of what was to become those developments in the Massachusetts of the Winthrops and Mathers, the developments which supplied the essential, distinguishing foundations of the United States of America, and which have provoked its greatest achievements to the advantage of all mankind since that time.

This brings our report thus far, to a crucial point. At this moment preceding, and still coinciding with the great, recurring world warfare of the A.D. 1890-1917 interval and beyond, the human civilization of this planet has presently come to what threatens to become immediately the extinction of human society in a recognizable form of existence.[6]

Despite that presently horrible threat now radiating across a vast span of history, since the spawn of the likes of the degenerate Roman Emperor Nero and his natural consequence, President Barack Obama's present master, the British monarchy, there are certain most notable features of the progress in physical science and Classical culture which have now reached a degree of cumulative development, a development which deserves to be regarded as the greatest accomplishments of the human species so far. Against that backdrop, what was embodied in European culture, despite the evil represented by that "Fourth" Roman Empire known as the British empire, has been the greatest achievement of mankind thus far. That specific accomplishment of resistance against the tyranny of today's British Empire, when appropriately considered, is the greatest hope of our planet and our species known to the entire existence of mankind up to this moment. We are, in that respect, the assigned true, and, hopefully, faithful, instruments of the Creator.

The most convenient point of reference to this fact, is a fact which is either not known as being such, or known, but snuffed into impotence by the evil stench of the mass- murderously anti-human pestilence known as the so-called "environmentalists."

Against that historical backdrop, the question posed to us by the world's current events, is whether mankind as we have known mankind has, or has had the charac-

ter to outlive what is to be frankly considered as the virtually Satanic pestilence which is the old Roman Empire in its present British imperial incarnation. Will the British empire be permitted to bring the planet to the point of that virtual thermonuclear extinction and related methods of extinction which a presently accelerating intention for mass-extermination of peoples by the British empire now threatens to bring down upon our species, that in its virtual entirety?

This fact places mankind, presently, under the judgment of being tested in practice to be either fit to survive, or not. If the British imperial plotters were to be permitted to prevail, the judgment brought down upon the heads of our otherwise wonderful species would be an awful one. What you, as a citizen, might do, or fail to do, could help to decide the outcome for all mankind.

Consider the attached, practical issues which are addressed in the following pages, on that account. There lies the choice of action which threatens to bring all to account during the present moments immediately before us.

From the practice of economy:

II. On the Subject of Economy

From where I sit in today's process of world events, what I find astonishing, is the fact, that the western and central European governments, and their attached nations, are still, so far, clinging to the delusion, that their nations depend on increasing their supply of what is, intrinsically, hyper-inflationary money, that which is now, implicitly worthless. Hence, also, there is more and more of that intrinsically worthless money of the United States under Presidents George W. Bush, Jr., on the one side, and on the other the morally lowest form of life to appear so far, Barack Obama, who is the most criminal yet to appear within our shores.

The debt of the trans-Atlantic territories today, is a hopeless cancer of inherently worthless, merely nominal, monetarist value, which does nothing so much as increase its own, intrinsic worthlessness at currently hyper-inflationary rates, all that out of a mass of worthless debt which never would, or ever could, be redeemed.

The stubbornly crucial fact of the matter, is, that money, when considered in and of itself, is, intrinsi-

---

6. The "World War" which was actually set into motion by the British Royal Family's 1890 ouster of Chancellor Bismarck, the subsequent 1894 assassination of France's President Sadi Carnot, and the pact British Crown Prince made with Japan's Mikado for launching war against China, Korea, and Russia over the period leading through 1905.

cally, absolutely irredeemable. The potential value lies not in the money itself (i.e., "monetarism"), but in the creative powers expressed in the human species' increased capacity for persistently increased net physical productivity, a productivity secured through combined advances in scientific knowledge and practice, and through enhanced cultural and related living standards for the populations in the large.

No actually sane political leader, or even only a moderately clear-headed and thoughtful citizen of our own republic, or of continental Europe, could have actually lost anything worth-while on this national account at this time, had his or her government simply employed the precedent of President Franklin Roosevelt's 1933 Glass-Steagall legislation, using that as the urgently needed step, for our terminating the implicitly feared existence of, in particular, those presently terrible, monetarist systems which had been built up within the U.S.A. and elsewhere, since approximately the Summer breaking-point of 1971.

What has been done for that which is now ever worse and far less than worthless, as inside the U.S.A. now, especially since the beginning of September 2007, and, most emphatically, since the mass-lunacy of the hyper-inflationary bail-out process begun in 2008, has been absolute insanity. In western and central Europe, for example, the insanity is even much wilder, and more hopeless, than inside the U.S.A. itself; this has become, now, the sheer insanity of what has been termed "Quantitative Easing"—which is a malignant cancer of economy now plunging the trans-Atlantic world downward, into the pits of virtual economic *Hell!*

The remedy for that should have been recognized at the outset, as follows.

My 2007 Attempt To Save the U.S. Economy

Installing a copy of the 1933 U.S. Glass-Steagall Law, or my August 2007 Homeowners and Bank Protection Act, or its proposed equivalent, had been an immediately urgent, first-step measure, which should have been already taken since no later than September 2007; but, that measure has been, at the same time, only a part of the larger measures of a solution for our present crisis. Glass-Steagall is necessary, but, alone, it could not do what is needed; it is urgently needed, right

EIRNS/James Rea

Adoption of LaRouche's Homeowners and Bank Protection Act of 2007, or today, a Glass-Steagall law, "is indispensable as a first step toward the now more urgently needed, more fundamental approaches to a genuine and durable recovery." Here, BüSo organizers in Berlin campaign for a return to the D-mark, and a two-tier banking system.

now, not as a self-contained solution, but is indispensable as a first step toward the now more urgently needed, more fundamental approaches to a genuine and durable recovery.

In brief, the practical problem has been the following.

Glass-Steagall separates the worthless spending on gambling backed by worthless pledges, from the commercial banking sector; the urgency of the immediate necessity for a change is such that the continued existence of the United States depends on the immediate ouster of President Barack Obama as the required, initially crucial measure for the launching of a Glass-Steagall reform. The amount of credit which could be assembled by Glass-Steagall alone, would not be sufficient to reverse the presently plunging collapse of the trans-Atlantic region as a whole, or even the U.S. economy by itself. A much broader action, which I shall specify here, now, is needed. There is not a moment to waste.

I explain.

Credit vs. Monetarist Systems

When the patriots of the North American English colonies had broken with the British empire, in the aftermath of the British Lord Shelburne's victory taken from the February 1763 Peace of Paris, the English-speaking colonies in North America had been divided between the American patriots and their deadly adversaries the so-called "American Tory" or British imperialist financier interests. The British East India Company's specific imperialist interest, as merely typified prominently by Judge Lowell at that time, represented the British imperialist interest opposed to the American interest (e.g., that of our United States), then, as in the form of the British imperialist interest now associated, traditionally, with the "House of Morgan," then, as now.

However, the proper understanding of the role of the British imperialist interests, requires insight into some deeper considerations. The British interest of today, is that of a nearly global empire which controls the Wall Street and related financier interests inside the U.S.A. still today, and has managed, usually, to control the Presidency of the United States, through the British imperial financier interests under such Presidents as Wall Street swindler Martin van Buren, and the patsy of van Buren, Andrew Jackson, who combined their efforts to wreck the finances of the United States through the combined actions of Jackson's, first, shutting down the Bank of the United States, and, then, van Buren's unleashing of the infamous (Bernanke-Geithner-style) swindle known as the Panic of 1837. Over the subsequent decades of the U.S. Presidency, most of the time, the President of United States has been an agent of the British empire working against the interest of the

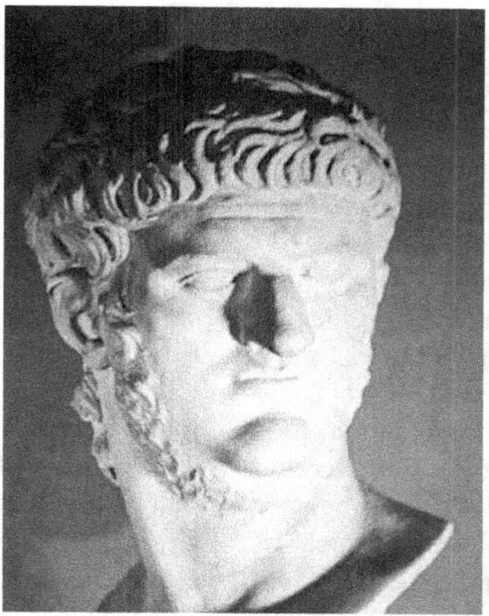

"There should be no mystery in the fact that U.S. President Barack Obama is, psychopathologically, a carbon copy of the Roman Emperor Nero."

United States and its Federal Constitution. Witness the recent cases of George H.W. Bush (the son of former Adolf Hitler backer Prescott Bush), of George W. Bush, Jr., and of the British monarchy's treasonous and murderous agent-in-fact, Barack Obama.

Such treasonous elements within the financier interests of the U.S. political system, are not simply bad people; they are intrinsically evil, currently witting agents of the present British empire under Queen Elizabeth II. More to the point, they have been agents of what is properly identified as the fourth categorical generation of the Roman empire, the actually dominant world empire in the world as a whole today. The kind of evil which that present British empire signifies today is not merely a matter of the virtual piracy and virtual slave-trading of the British system today. The essential characteristic of that British empire, like all Europe-centered empires of all ancient through modern history, is a characteristic which is common to not only the successive incarnations of the Roman Empire, including today's present British incarnation of that empire; but to the powerful empires which had played a dominant role prior to the foundation of the original Roman empire.

The essence of all such empires as those has been what is called "the oligarchical system," the system which is characteristic of the monetarist financial/banking systems of the trans-Atlantic system and its broader correlatives. The rape of what had once been the economies and nations of western and central Europe under the pretext of the so-called "Euro system" is nothing but the suppression of the former sovereign nations of those parts of Europe, to replace them by transforming them into the powerless colonies of the nominally British form of the modern Roman Empire.

The principal characteristics of the Roman empire, its predecessors and sequels, is what is aptly typified by both Homer's account of the Trojan War, and by the continuing cult of Apollo (The Oracle of Delphi), and by the accounts of the aftermath of the Trojan War which had been presented, later, by the chronicler and dramatist Aeschylus. These particular cases, together with the legacy of the Roman Empire, are typical of what is known technically by relevant experts as "the oligarchical system."

The "oligarchical system" divides the human populations between what were designated, explicitly, as being "the gods," and, on the other side, the slaves or serfs. That same system, with certain relatively superficial changes, has been the social system reigning over Europe to the present time of the ongoing breakdown-crisis throughout virtually all of the present trans-Atlantic region.

Thus, there should be no mystery in the fact, that U.S. President Barack Obama is, psychopathologically, a carbon copy of the Roman Emperor Nero. Read the facts about Obama; you are reading a carbon copy of the mental and moral degeneracies which are characteristic of the Emperor Nero. If you support Obama in the Presidency today, you are supporting a living carbon copy of the mass-murderous butcher known to history as the Emperor Nero, or as the similarly pathological personality of the dictator Adolf Hitler. It was not the war which made Hitler a copy of Nero; it was the outbreak of war which unleashed what had been the potential inside Hitler all along, as the case of Nero presents similar features to the case of Hitler. Obama is, within himself, actually worse than Hitler, unless you remove him from office, under Section "4" of the Twenty-Fifth Amendment to the U.S. Constitution, right now!

However, with certain notable exceptions, such as the domain of Charlemagne and his friend Caliph Haroun al-Raschid, the characteristic of what is known as the culture of Europe and its neighboring regions, has been the same oligarchical principle known to us from such precedents as the Peloponnesian War, all the way up to the eruption of Europe's Fifteenth-century Renaissance. Most notable on this account had been the Renaissance's role as centered in the Great Ecumenical Council of Florence, and the emergence of a modern European civilizing thrust radiated chiefly from the effects of the Great Council, as typified by the career and outcomes associated with Cardinal Nicholas of Cusa, including the principal foundations of all competent strains of modern European science and art.

Amid this, since the brutish English monarchy of King Henry VIII, there had been a literally Hellish raging of religious warfare throughout European civilization as such. The principled issue has been the combat of a humanist culture traced from the high points of the Great Ecumenical Council of Florence, against the recrudesence of the ancient evil of the oligarchical pestilence. Since the emergence of the Sarpian New Venetian party of William of Orange built up around the Netherlands Wars against the France of a foolish Louis XIV, and the subsequent Seven Years War which established an actual British Empire, Europe's wars have been a monstrous evil crafted in the tradition of the ancient Roman Empire and of that Empire's likenesses as Byzantium, the Venetian-controlled Crusader adventures, and the emergence of the British Empire of today.

The most often recognized characteristic of the evil which is the present British Empire, lies in the central significance of its monetarist system. The facts, if considered, were readily clear; but, for most people today (even today), true facts concerning money and money-systems are not interesting in much of any fashion but a gambler's foolish lust.

Money, as money or its likeness, has no actual economic value. The problem here is that with the creation of a monopoly over money, either by a nation-state, or some potency which exerts a private monopoly over a public currency, the fact that money becomes a monopoly of the ruling political power, under such as our rotted-out Federal Reserve System (by the House of Morgan's legacy) and its Wall Street and London attachments, or the International Monetary Fund, which uses a strangle-hold over the public use of money in such a way, including creation of hyperinflationary bubbles of London and Wall Street, using dearth of money, or an hyperinflationary surfeit, to control money in such a fashion as to exert life-death controls over the very existence of the general population.

I have been forecasting with what has been consistent success (on principle) since my Summer 1956 fore-

" 'Quantitative Easing' is, intrinsically, the most insane, most stupid, but also the most larcenous swindle which any modern, simply madman-government might have committed, placing its foolish trust in intrinsically ever-worthless fictitious debt conceived in emulation of the 1923 debt of Weimar Germany." Shown: "The Moneylender and His Wife," Quentin Massys (1514).

cast of a severe U.S. recession to break out some time between the close of February 1957, or no later than early March. All among the forecasts I have actually published since that 1957 event, have been uniquely successful; whereas, all those of all my known putative rivals have failed in their performance, up to the present time. The failures of my putative rivals in forecasting have been also consistent. The fact of the matter is, that my rivals' policies respecting the nature of such developments, have been consistently based on wrong, monetarist presumptions. They have been dupes of that which they have been induced to believe, right up to the present moment.

What has been wrong about them, has been their refusal to understand the meaning of money as being no better than the quality of physical-economic value intrinsic to the purpose for which the credit is extended;

money as such has no intrinsic value. Virtually all of their principal assumptions have been failures; this is because they have failed to understand the nature of the oligarchical system which they have been induced to accept.

This history is not merely a matter of personal tyrannical destinies. The root of the evil is located in a cancer-like disease known formally as the same oligarchical principle chronicled by Homer on the subject of the Trojan War. It has been the oligarchical form of control of the creation and use of money, which is the essential cause of all catastrophic failures of money systems as under the influence of a Morgan tradition's London-based asset, Alan Greenspan, which ruined the U.S. economy since the early 1980s. The issue to be treated, lies in the fact of that oligarchical principle whose principal representation for today is the British empire of Queen Elizabeth II. Defeat that empire, or, by negligence of your duty, you will imagine that you are rotting in Hell—if you live long enough to understand that.

I will say more on this matter of money in the following chapter of this present report.

III. Fool's Gold, Et Al.

As this just-stated fact is demonstrated by the effects of the wild-eyed speculation which money represents throughout and around so much of the world today: money itself never actually expressed either an intrinsic quality, or a quantity of "economic value" within any economy from around the world; that is especially the matter to come under our attention under the present conditions in the trans-Atlantic regions. "Quantitative Easing" is, intrinsically, the most insane, most stupid, but also the most larcenous swindle which any modern, simply madman-government might have committed, placing its foolish trust in intrinsically ever-worthless fictitious debt conceived in emulation of the 1923 debt of Weimar Germany.

That is the judgment to be made on, for example, the far worse than Weimar worthlessness, of the implicitly hyperinflationary succession of both the George W. Bush, Jr. and Obama governments—not to speak here of the present situation in western and central Europe. Whether the attributed wealth is denominated in dollars, pound sterling, or anything of the like: those governments, like their British imperial accomplices, would be, and have been viciously insane by virtue of that fact alone. Actual wealth exists only as a rising rate of what is expressed as net gains in physical benefits generated as increased physical productivity to mankind per capita and per square kilometer, as that might be measured as a rising rate of physical gain per day and per person, to meet the current needs of mankind, and for progress, per person, and with the passage of time.

This sometimes seemingly miraculous power, the power to increase the production of physical wealth, per capita and per square kilometer of territory, is obtained, if at all, chiefly through the uniqueness of the willful, conscious powers to effect the increase of the uniquely human powers of the equivalent of physical-scientific creativity per capita and per square kilometer of territory; or this may be expressed in terms of the increase of mankind's power to rise from the surface of our home planet, to higher altitudes above the immediate surface of the Earth, as in a successful round-trip, to and from the Moon, or Mars.

Thus, it was only during the early 1950s, that, through the effect of bringing on the development of space-exploration and comparable kinds of development, that our society had come to recognize an actual, practical insight into what is to be considered comparable to reaching the highest altitudes enveloping our planet's surface regions. More recently, those persons who have been competently informed in matters of science, have come to recognize that even the weather experienced by the inhabitants of our planet, is not independent of effects controlled by such relatively nearby "weather" as the arms of our galaxy.

Not only must we be responsive to changes in such reaches of galactic "weather;" but, unless human life on our planet suffers massive destruction, such as by thermonuclear warfare, or comparable effects, we shall certainly be called upon to deal with what will include highly unfriendly patterns of actual weather within our galaxy, a threat from such "weather" which we must become enabled to conquer in a timely fashion, over the course of unfolding times to come during later generations of this young century.

So, in the estimated, approximately half-billion years of the presently known historical evidence of the history of life on Earth, the existence of life on Earth, has required an increase of the available "energy-flux density" of the density of power[7] required to maintain human life on and near the surface of our planet, even during the recent several millions of years of the fairly assessed increase of human life on Earth. To the best of our present knowledge, the human species is the only species which commands the willful powers to approach its needed rates of increase specific to the human population, that done through willfully creative powers. We have much to happen which will become new for us over times to come, but those categorical characteristics of the human species's destiny are presently known to us, as a sense of the role of a principle of change on which the existence of human life continues to depend.

What we might consider as the possible increases in man's power to exist and grow over the coming generations of this presently young century, as we have had such experiences from the model, past two centuries of our history, is the expression of what we also know as the suggested possible increase of the productive powers of labor, down here, on Earth. This should be a reasonable expectation in light of the fact of that deep, willfully self-inflicted depression in the physical economy which has hit the trans-Atlantic sector of the world, a depression associated with the correlatives of the assassinations of John F. Kennedy and his brother Robert, and, also, the effects of the related, long U.S. war in Indo-China. The combination of the failure of the U.S. to take competent action against those assassinations, and the insanity of entering into such disturbances as a prolonged war in Southeast Asia, were the essential causes which set off what has been, since, the long, accelerating decline within the trans-Atlantic economy.

A Mental Disorder Called "Money"

Throughout what had been the extensive prefatory feature of this report as a combined whole, one common irony pervades all truthfully defined effects. The extent of all truly human systems is self-defined as within the

---

7. E.g., "energy-flux density."

extensible regions of mankind's willful influence within the galaxy, man-made functioning gadgets included, rather than by a measure arbitrarily super-imposed from without.

That is the extent of the true human economy, in the past, as now. The same is true for any competent notion of "value" in the practice of physical economy. The internal measure of our universe, as is implicit in the physical-economic standard of the equivalent of "energy-flux density" per capita, reflects the notion of a general conceptual basis for the proper notion of the internal discipline of a self-contained universe, and of mankind's presently, and irrevocably, extra-terrestrially extended "world" economy.

Now, consider some other critical features of mankind's economy. Forget Barack Obama's views on such matters; after all, there is no reasonable doubt that he is insane, and that is to be considered as criminal insanity under any reasonable estimate of Section 4 of the Twenty-Fifth Amendment to our U.S. Constitution: much more "criminal"in terms of the rate of increase of presently embedded effects of his reign to date, than Adolf Hitler and his crew.

The popularized idea of "money" is of crucial importance as a destructive influence on the economy and its population. Neither gold bullion nor any other standard external to the process of the correlative notion of an increase of energy-flux density, need be sought outside what we might define, in practical terms, as the limitless self-development of a finite but unbounded universe, like that intended by Albert Einstein.

It is the process of what is, in effect, the increase of the energy-flux density of human activity within our universe, which measures mankind actually. Neither gold, nor any other object, but what is represented as mankind, or as a comparable form of agency internal to the universal system, really means much of anything in the proverbial "final analysis."

The Frauds of Laplace

The crucial issue posed by the remarks which I had just presented, immediately above, is what is typified, symptomatically, by the need to exclude the absurd doctrine of what is called "time" by those sharing the foolish beliefs of a Pierre-Simon Laplace. Here lie the most crucial aspects of the lunacy of Laplace's dubious

It is the process of what is, in effect, the increase of the energy-flux density of human activity within our universe, which measures mankind actually.

assertions respecting the physical authority of widely taught contemporary mathematics as such. I summarize my argument in this present chapter by re-stating the direction of the argument which I have made at earlier points of time in this present report, up to this present point. The intrinsic absurdity of Laplace's cardinal assertions is manifold; I shall tear apart Laplace's hoax, as if "piece by piece," in the extent necessary, accordingly, here and now.

First of all, I shall return to the implications of some of Laplace's design which point blatantly to what is the intrinsic nature of the fraud he has perpetrated by the blatantly fraudulent approach to the definition of "time" as such. He locates the existence of what he identifies as "time" outside the universe, thus echoing, in that way, the clear absurdity of a similarly fraudulent notion of "space by itself." These related notions, of "time by itself" and "space by itself," are part of the most essential of the outright frauds against the very essence of science, which are associated with the attributably systemic intentions of Laplace. The worst of all of his frauds is his errant reliance on a notion of "time by itself," as being also, implicitly, the absurdity of "time and space for itself."

All that could be reasonably considered as competent physical science, and not that of perverted creatures such as Bertrand Russell, is premised on clear evidence of the necessarily, actively consistent interdependence of any general form of ontological claims respecting the definition of the characteristics of actions within that universe which contains and defines even the very hypothesis of "time per se." What is left to be believed, is the notion of a remaining, systemically persistent notion of "physical time," a notion which was already implicit in Johannes Kepler's uniquely original concept of universal gravitation which is situated within Albert Einstein's notion of a Keplerian universe which is "finite, but not bounded."

Within the bounds of those immediately aforesaid specifications, the progress of science thus far, has been afforded two principal options, the contrast among which, enables civilized mankind at the level of a presently assignable standard for approaching a precondition of approximate certainty in those matters, a sense of certainty which should be currently attributable to the principled matters of what is to be regarded currently as competent science. The one is human "sense perception;" the alternative is what may be usefully classified as the general electrodynamics of physical time (rather than "clock time") within the universe, that insofar as we are enabled, increasingly, practically, to broaden our efficient reach within that domain.

The currently most useful manner for stating that case, is implicitly stated in the view of the work of Bernhard Riemann from the standpoint of such as what is underlain by the contributions of such among Riemann's excellent followers as Max Planck, Albert Einstein, and V.I. Vernadsky. It is through that inter-play among the exemplary contributions of those three, that science has been presently enabled to present a decent effort at creating solutions which threaten to overcome the enormous debt of irrationality which we incur by seeking to derive a science from the currently relatively "popular" presumptions respecting human sense-perception in and of itself.

That, however, which I have stated thus far, is not yet more than the beginning of the extent of what is presently of crucial importance that society come to know presently. Shift our emphasis, slightly, to take into account a crucial statement of scientific fact which I presented summarily, in replies to two questions presented to me during the concluding part of my report delivered to a September 20, 2011 national webcast. That was the public event during which I broadcast a report of the scientific meaning of a general scientific principle of human economic productivity. The evidence presented on that occasion, sinks Laplace's a-priorist assertions respecting time permanently: it simply shows that Laplace presented no credible evidence for his notion of time as a phenomenon in the universe as such.[8]

Laplace's Time Spent in Empty Space

How could Laplace have counted time while observing from the interior of empty space? Against what phenomenon could one have counted time in empty space? If there were no suitable clock used for that purpose, how, when, or where was "time" countable as elapsed time? How could a duration of lapsed "time" be measured in terms of that allegedly, actually empty "space" which Laplace has claimed as his own intellectual residence?

There are several choices for response to such a hoax as Laplace's.

The likely attempted answer to the challenge which I have just delivered (in a timely fashion) here, is that if we exclude space, action, and matter from the hypothetical universe, what is the meaning of "time by itself?"

That just stated consideration, stands by itself, as Laplace, implicitly, said as much, himself. How long could a Laplace have been justly assigned to serve in an actual prison on a charge of fraud against, among notable others, clock-makers? In an actually empty space, there are no minutes which could have been countable.

Unfortunately for Laplace's tattered claims to scientific fame, empty space does not exist, either. At bottom, there is no ontological basis for the universe other than creativity per se. Laplace sits in empty space, knitting without yarn, or, needles, either. See! What a spectacle he would have made, had he been visible, somewhere! Today, somewhere in Hell, there sits Laplace knitting, whispering furiously under his breath, but to no one: "Gottfried Leibniz is dead!" So claimed the pack of scoundrels led by the Abbé Antonio Schinella Conti (1677-1749), who virtually created his protégé Isaac Newton out of some curious substance, as that same Conti found such accomplices in fraud as another fabricator of crude hoaxes, Leonhard Euler (also against Gottfried Leibniz), and also other errand-boys for the legacy of Paolo Sarpi, who had tried to bury Leibniz (once they had been assured that Leibniz had just recently died). Laplace's place in the history of frauds perpetrated in the alleged service of science, is also to be found in the continuation of that same anti-Leibniz cabal as among one of Laplace's own errand-boys. It is therefore not surprising that every one of Newton's claims for scientific fame was exposed in due course as an utter hoax, and all depending inclusively on the hoaxes of Conti and his accomplices.

IV. A System of Physical Economy

A competent system for today's modern science of physical economy, is a practice chiefly based on a systemic method of contrast between two, contrasted methods of calculations. The first, *the subjective method*, had been premised, chiefly, on an acceptance

---

8. I had, in fact, already stated the relevant principle in several published locations.

"Since human knowledge depends upon the link of the physical to the mental life of the human individual . . . the most significant of the qualitative advances in human behavior must originate outside sense-perception, as the celebrated case of Helen Keller points our attention." Shown: Helen Keller "reading."

of human sense-perception; the second, *the objective method*, was premised, chiefly, on what is most easily recognized in the use of modern electronics as a substitute for sense-perception. The optimal net result is a contrast defined by both the interaction and opposition between those two categories of perceptions.

Since human knowledge, as such, depends upon that link of the physical to the mental life of the human individual, a mental life which is moored in the use of the human brain for the management of the traffic in products of sense-perception, the most significant of the qualitative advances in human behavior must originate outside sense-perception as the celebrated case of Helen Keller points our attention.

However, a competent insight into the physical domain depends, centrally, upon the recognition of the evidence of the system of the phenomena of what might be fairly identified as the "electro-chemical" domain. The reciprocal aspects of the two so-indicated domains, are functionally inter-dependent. That interaction is the

experimental basis in knowledge for the gaining of human progress. It is the promotion of the human individual's socialized processes of development of such a systemic approach, which must be the center of our concerns.

From the attributable "beginnings," it has been the contrast among mankind's specific types of sense-perceptions which generated the paradoxes on which the derivation of the notion of principles, rather than merely contrasted sensations, has depended. Out of this comes the notion of sense-perception as "subjective," and the rest as "objective." The human mind in society tends to seek the human side as "subjective" and the electronic, et al., as the "objective." The two sides, then, "teach" one another.[9]

The most crucial of the related facts to be considered, is the ostensibly, ontologically paradoxical challenge represented by the notion of "human individual creativity." Suddenly, with the intervention of the notion of "human individual creativity," all preceding presumptions crumble in a way which it becomes frighteningly difficult to resist; a threat of an imminent sense of "falling," becomes the sense which it is often terrifyingly difficult to resist.

The person frightened by the prospect of such an experience, not-infrequently reacts to that by falling into a relatively brutish reaction (e.g., the scream of wild-eyed denial: "that's nuts!") against any intimations of actual human creativity. "You are attempting to invade me!" The latter phenomenon was demonstrated against truly great scientists, largely through the criminality of Bertrand Russell, or of the apparent "idiot-savant," John von Neumann, against Albert Einstein, et al., in the course of major scientific assemblies of the 1920s and later.

The crucial point to be emphasized in conclusion here, is that a real economy is a physical economy, an economy whose efficient intent includes the urgent need for high-energy-flux-density, capital-intensive, science-driver programs of development and investments, of the types which shall continue to be the emphasis of my efforts during the foreseeable times to come.

---

9. Again, on this subject, reference the concluding section #3 of Bernhard Riemann's habilitation dissertation, and, implicitly, his ***Theory of Abelian Functions***.

Leibniz from LaRouche's Standpoint

by Ernest Schapiro

by Ernest Schapiro

INTRODUCTION
The Study of Historical Specificity Leads to the Higher Hypothesis

It is not widely appreciated that Lyndon LaRouche has founded a new theory of knowledge, namely that the truth of a Platonic idea—an immaterial physical principle—is only to be determined by situating that idea within a historical series of such ideas, and deducing what is common to them all, despite their uniquely individual historically specific content. More specifically than that, the validity of these ideas is demonstrated by their contribution to our ability to increase the potential population density of the society and of the planet as a whole. In Changing the Universe-A Philosophy of Victory, he tells us that he developed this strategy of defining the higher hypothesis bounding and subsuming an historical series of hypotheses, in the early 1950's as he began to look at the succession of ancient Greek playwrights, poets, and philosophers and began defining their successive hypotheses—Plato being the last and most advanced thinker of the series starting with Homer. He recognized that to understand any one of them you had to understand the principle of revolutionary axiomatic change that led from each of them to the next.[1]

Homer

Parmenides

Plato

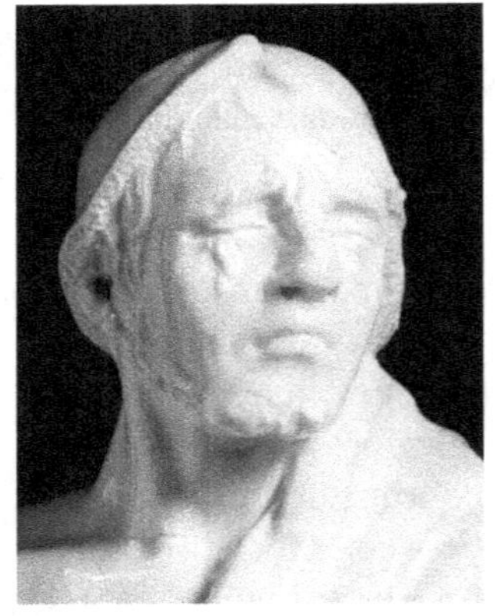
Heraclitus

Autobiographically: during 1951, the puzzle posed by the similarities and differences between the import of the known fragments attributed to Heraclitus, and the clarity of Plato's argument on the ontological implications of "becoming," prompted a crucial turn, at that time, in my own approach to the problems of a science of physical economy. The qualitative differences among the Homeric outlook, the pre-Socratic thinkers, that of the classical tragedians, and Plato's dialogues, must be appreciated if any useful knowledge for modern use is to be adduced from the study of the work of any among them. If a reader were curious as to where I developed the passion for historical specificity

---

1. Lyndon H. LaRouche, Jr., *The Economics of the Noösphere*, Executive Intelligence Review, 2001. See pages 116-122 for comments about Platonic ideas.

which I stress here, the answer is implicitly provided to him in the present location.[2]

I believe the crucial turn he is referring to was his discovery that the physical aspect of all economies is subject to an invariant principle or law, the series of such invariants being analogous to a series of hypotheses, which are subject to a common higher hypothesis.[3]

The invariant law was the requirement for a surplus of free energy, or negative entropy, over and above what was needed to maintain the status quo, a surplus violating the so-called Second Law of Thermodynamics. This growth process must have an exponential tendency.[4] He arrived at this invariant law after a rigorous study of the succession of economies back to ancient times.

However he also saw a second invariant principle historically specific to capitalism, the general rate of profit.[5] This was the "subjective" side of the economy, emphasizing "exchange value" as opposed to "use value," i.e. how the society views its own activity. In the last chapter of **Dialectical Economics**, "The Great Fugue," he elaborates

G.W. Leibniz
(1646-1716)

the way in which the interaction of these two optimizing principles, each acting cyclically, played out over the post World War II period. The interaction of these two principles led to boundary conditions and singularities, i.e. general breakdown crises of the society, such as the crisis the trans-Atlantic nations are now undergoing.

The ideology of a society is its hypothesis or axiomatic structure.

In order to account for specific subordinate ideologies within the general ideology, we need only recognize that the invariant of capitalist accumulation is not directly expressed to each group in the same way. The invariant generates a variety of special sub-characteristics, more or less in the same way that postulates determine theorems, causing occupants of different regions of capitalist space to see the whole in terms of pseudo-invariants, or "special laws." Yet while the immediate characteristics of consciousness may differ among social strata, the "hereditary" feature of the general principle embedded in the "special laws," is adducible from individuals "conscious" and "unconscious" behavior.[6]

LaRouche's uniquely proven ability to forecast is based on this complex understanding of what he called the "dialectical" interaction of the two optimizing principles, a conflict being mediated by the historically determined consciousness of the population. I believe this understanding benefitted from his study of Leibniz.

Leibniz spoke often of the two kingdoms: the kingdom of power or efficient causes, analogous to the

____

2. "LaRouche's Discovery", **Fidelio,** Spring, 1994. See especially the section "The Theory of Knowledge." In **The Economics of the Noösphere**, see the section starting on page 106, "The Problem of Historical Specificity," through page 115. Especially, see footnote page 113. See also Lyn Marcus, Dialectical Economics, (Lexington, Mass.: D.C. Heath and Company, 1975), for numerous references to historical specificity.

3. **Dialectical Economics** pp.136-139 and the chapter "Feudalism to Capitalism."

4. **Dialectical Economics**, page 47, on the subject of an exponential tendency.

5. See Dialectical Economics for numerous references to the general rate of profit and the paradox of the falling rate of profit which accompanies capitalist crises. To my knowledge, LaRouche is the only economist to solve this paradox.

____

6. **Dialectical Economics**, p. 60.

physical economy, and the kingdom of final causes, the latter being analogous to how the society defines its activity, both its social processes and its relationship to nature.

In his ground breaking treatise on dynamics, **Specimen Dynamicum**, Leibniz says:

In fact, as I have shown by the remarkable example of the principle of optics, the celebrated Molyneux having warmly approved my interpretation in his **Dioptrics**, final causes may be introduced with great fruitfulness, even into the special problems of physics, not merely to increase our admiration for the most beautiful works of the supreme author, but also to help us make predictions by means of them which might not be as apparent, except perhaps hypothetically, through the use of efficient causes. Philosophers in the past have perhaps not sufficiently observed this advantage of final causes. It must be maintained in general that all existent facts can be explained in two ways—through a kingdom of *power* or *efficient causes* and through a kingdom of wisdom or *final causes*; that God regulates bodies as machines in an architectural manner according to laws of *magnitude* or *mathematics* but does so for the benefit of souls, and that he rules over souls, on the other hand, which are capable of wisdom, as over citizens and members of the same society with himself, in the manner of a prince or indeed of a father, ruling to his own glory according to the *Laws of Goodness* or *of Morality*. Thus these two kingdoms everywhere permeate each other, yet their laws are never confused and never disturbed, so that the maximum in the kingdom of power, and the best in the kingdom of wisdom, take place together. But here we have undertaken to set up the general rules for effective forces, which we can then use in explaining special efficient causes.[7]

Thus, in his writings on economics, Leibniz placed great emphasis on both the intrinsic moral and physical principles involved in economy, including the fact that unlike a mere beast, a worker's productivity requires an adequate and appropriate standard of living and a healthy cognitive environment in the work place.[8] He collaborated with Denis Papin in developing the first steam engine, which Papin said could allow one man to do the work of one hundred.[9] However LaRouche's second invariant, the general rate of monetary profit, was not relevant to the pre capitalist economy of his day, which lacked financial markets linked through central banking. Leibniz's view is in stark contrast to the view that economics, "the dismal science," is the domain of "objective laws," whether these laws are based on supply and demand or on a labor theory of value. His voluntaristic outlook thoroughly determined his view of both the moral and physical universe. Thus after elaborating his theory of pre-established harmony, he said:

There is to be discovered in it also this great advantage that instead of saying that we are free only in appearance in a way sufficient for practical life, as several intelligent persons have believed, we should rather say that we are determined only in appearance but in strict metaphysical language we are perfectly independent relatively to the influence of all other creatures. This again puts in a marvelous light the immortality of our soul and the constantly uniform conservation of our individuality, perfectly regulated by its own nature, protected from all external accidents, notwithstanding any appearance to the contrary. Never has a system put our elevation in greater evidence. Every mind being like a world apart, sufficient unto itself, independent of any other creature, containing the infinite, expressing the universe, is as enduring, as subsistent, and as absolute as the very universe of creatures.[10]

7. Leibniz, **Philosophical Papers and Letters**, Volume 2 Second Edition (D. Reidel Publishing Company, 1976). Leibniz, **Specimen Dynamicum** (Leroy Loemker, Editor), page 442.

8. "Leibniz, Society and Economy," **Fidelio,** Fall, 1992.

9. Philip Valenti, "Leibniz, Papin and the Steam Engine: A Case Study of British Sabotage of Science," **Fusion**, December, 1979 or http://www.schillerinstitute.org/educ/pedagogy/steam_engine.html

10. "New System of Nature and of the Communication of Substances, as Well as the Union of Body and Soul, 1695," in **Leibniz: Selections**. Edited by Philip P. Wiener (New York: Charles Scribner's Sons, 1951). Also in Loemker, page 453.

Both LaRouche and Leibniz placed great stress on Natural Law, i.e. universal principles which are knowable through creative reason and which therefore predictably govern the effects of our social and physical economic practice. This notion of a higher law is opposed to the Thomas Hobbes-Newt Gingrich "social contract," based on false, lying *a priori* assertions about the nature of man. Through natural law, a society based upon false and immoral principles will bring destruction upon itself without God having to intervene. Thus, what Leibniz referred to as "natural theology," as in the opening lunge of his first letter in the debate with Clarke, was an aspect of natural law.[11]

In LaRouche's Discovery paper, he says: "All along, there are certain virtually absolute social truths, with the force of *Natural Law*, embedded in the cumulative evidence of the historically successful Platonic higher hypothesis." He proceeds to enumerate three such truths, in a manner very reminiscent of Leibniz's writings on natural law, particularly Leibniz's view of what constitutes wisdom, happiness, and justice and the proper ordering of society to maximally achieve those ends for every individual. Leibniz's notion of freedom is the freedom to do good, rather than freedom to act upon one's idiosyncratic impulses. The exercise of this freedom was what the American founding fathers called "the pursuit of happiness."[12] Both Leibniz and LaRouche define the good we do as our access to immortality. The emergence of the sovereign nation state based on the common good in the 15th Century expressed natural law.

To sum up this introduction, I have come to the conclusion that something LaRouche and Leibniz have

Lyndon H. LaRouche, Jr.

uniquely in common is the view that freedom is not only a necessary good for human progress, but that it expresses a universal physical principle present in all domains: the cognitive or social, the biological, and the non-living. This emerges with Leibniz's notion of the monad. Furthermore, it is to be found from the microphysical or subatomic out to the astrophysical dimension. I think one can usefully compare LaRouche's idea of a "strong hypothesis," simultaneously applicable to all of those domains, to a higher hypothesis which subsumes an historical series of hypotheses, each with its necessary predecessor.

Solving Paradoxes of the One and the Many: Axiomatic Revolutionary Change in One's Mathematics as Higher Hypothesis

In his papers "LaRouche's Discovery" and "Leibniz from Riemann's Standpoint," LaRouche discusses his debts to Riemann and to Leibniz, his debt to Leibniz being far greater. LaRouche says that dragons guard the secrets of nature. To make his discovery in physical economy, he had to reject the universally accepted Second Law of Thermodynamics, as applied to the universe as a whole, to the biosphere, and to a physical economy. Only then could he conceive of a society that generates a net surplus of free energy required to increase population density and productivity per capita. Had he not read and understood the deeper meaning of Leibniz's attack on Newton at the beginning of the Leibniz-Clarke debate, concerning the clock-winder paradox, he could not have gotten past the dragons, nor challenged Norbert Wiener's statistical or informational notion of anti-entropy.

In the "LaRouche's Discovery" paper, LaRouche gets at the root of Newton's self entrapment in the clock winder paradox, namely his choice of mathematics,

---

11. By natural theology he meant theology which could be demonstrated through creative reason, not requiring revelation.

12. Robert Trout, "Life Liberty and the Pursuit of Happiness: How the *Natural Law* concept of G.W. Leibniz Inspired America's Founding Fathers, Fidelio, Vol. 6, Number 1, Spring, 1997".

Nicholas of Cusa
(1401-1464)

which is necessarily also a choice of physical assumptions. Newton's physics is an expression of his mathematics and vice versa. It is the belief in discrete things as primary, separated by empty space and interacting percussively or by "forces" over a distance. From this axiomatic standpoint, matter is that which is discrete, and its repeated division ends in an ultimate particle. Newton himself admitted that this was his method when he acknowledged that action at a distance was an absurdity.[13]

This choice of mathematics was also at the root of Archimedes' erroneous belief that one could construct a plane figure precisely equal to the area of a circle by trapping the circle between an infinite series of polygons inside and outside the circle. Cusa proved for the first time that π was neither a rational nor an irrational number, but in fact a new type of number, and that the circle subsumed the plane figures composed of straight lines and points.[14] In so doing he rejected Euclidean geometry, which axiomatically begins with lines and points, not the circle, and uses rotation of the line to produce a circle. This is not a dead issue. It is the reason Cusa's priority in discovering the transcendental nature of π is to this day not acknowledged. The real issue is

Cusa's non-inductive resort to a method of hypothesis, a kind of non-inductive leap.[15] Denial of nonlinearity in the small is the root of Leonhard Euler's attack on Leibniz's monads, based on the tautology of assuming infinite divisibility, the very thing Euler needed to prove.[16] It is the root of Cauchy's epsilon-delta ritual to smooth out the curve as one approaches a "limit," by which he destroyed the physical implication of Leibniz's differential calculus.[17]

LaRouche personally had rejected Euclidean geometry in his first classroom encounter with it, before encountering Leibniz.[18] What he derived from Leibniz is succinctly expressed by Leibniz in 1697 in *The Radical Origination of Things*.

In addition to the beauties and perfections of the totality of the divine works, we must also recognize a certain constant and unbounded progress in the whole universe, so that it always proceeds to greater development, just as a large portion of our world is now cultivated and will become more and more so. And while certain things regress to their original wild state and others are destroyed and buried, we must, however, understand this in the same way that we interpreted affliction a bit earlier. Indeed, this very destruction and burying leads us to the attainment of something better, so that we make a profit from the very loss, in a sense.

And there is a ready answer to the objection that if this were so, then the world should have become paradise a long time ago. Many sub-

---

13. For Newton quote, See the online **Stanford Encyclopedia of Philosophy**, 2006 Revised 2014, Section 5: "The Aftermath of the Principia. I. Relations with John Locke and Richard Bentley."
14. William F. Wertz, "Quadrature of the Circle," **Fidelio**, Summer 2001.

15. Lyndon LaRouche, "How Bertrand Russell Became an Evil Man," **Fidelio**, Fall 1994. In Part III, Section (g) of the online version, LaRouche analyzes in detail the case of Felix Klein, and what led Klein to perpetrate a fraud in omitting the priority of Cusa.
16. Lyndon LaRouche, **The Science of Christian Economy** (Washington: Schiller Institute, 1991), pages 407-425, for some of Euler's letters and LaRouche's comments. Also see **Twenty First Century Science and Technology**, Winter 1995-96, LaRouche, "Riemann Refutes Euler."
17. Ernest Schapiro, "The Real Calculus Versus What You Learned," **21st Century Science & Technology**, Fall 1999. Especially see attacks on Leibniz's calculus by Charles Boyer and Richard Courant.
18. Lyndon LaRouche, "Economics as History," **EIR**, Sept. 18, 2009.

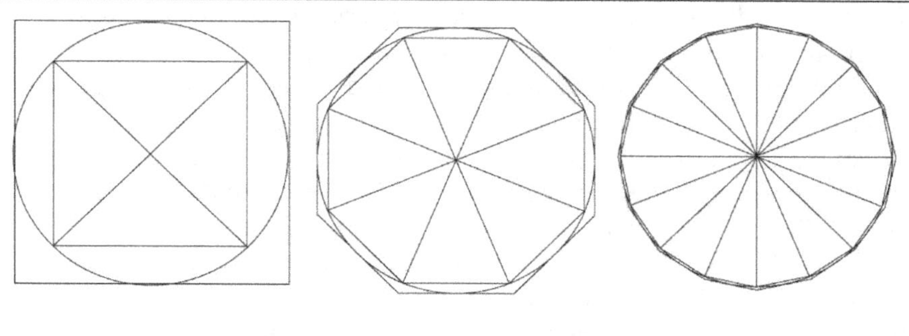

Nicholas of Cusa showed that Archimedes' attempt at "quadrature of the circle"—to approximate the value of pi—was ontologically incompetent. The first three drawings show the process of estimating the area of a square approximately equa; to that of a given circle, as the average area of two regular polygons. In the last drawing, although the inscribed polygon of 216 may seem to closely approximate a circle in area, it actually contains a devastating paradox. There are slightly more than 182 angles of the inscribed polygon within each degree of circular arc.

stances have already attained great perfection. However, because of the infinite divisibility [Leibniz's "worlds within worlds," not Euler's idea of infinite divisibility—E.S.] of the continuum, there are always parts asleep in the abyss of things, yet to be roused and yet to be advanced to greater and better things, advanced, in a word, to greater cultivation. Thus progress never comes to an end."[19]

In LaRouche's own similarly optimistic view, the universe as a negentropic continuum generates singularities of progressively higher power.[20]

The universe is governed by creativity and is alive. Since this applies no matter how small what you are considering is, there can be no linearity in the small.

LaRouche credits Riemann with taking Leibniz's ideas to a higher level. For example he used Leibniz's ideas of the universal characteristic and *analysis situs* to construct a succession of multiply extended manifolds, each subsuming and of a higher order than its predecessors of fewer dimensions. In going from the lower to the higher manifold, i.e. from n to n+1 dimensions, one encountered a discontinuous change in curvature or metric for the manifold as a whole.[21] La-

Rouche says that it was because he had intensively studied Leibniz's **Monadology** in his adolescence that he could compare Riemann's system with Leibniz's ordering of monads (or singularities) of increasingly higher power. Thus, LaRouche says that his own work in physical economy has increased the authority of Riemann, because LaRouche has replaced Riemann's manifold of independent dimensions with a manifold of independent interacting physical principles, and shown its applicability to physical economy. Each new principle finds expression via the machine tool principle, in new technologies, operating in a new Riemannian manifold, that increases our productivity and population density.

Such a succession of hypotheses, governed by axiomatic revolutionary change, could begin with Plato's Parmenides dialogue. Plato humorously shows that the only solution to the many formal paradoxes presented by the Eleatic philosophers, Parmenides and Zeno, is to introduce the principle of change, which LaRouche further characterizes as going to a new hypothesis, an axiomatic revolutionary change.[22]

As already cited, nearly 2000 years later, Nicholas of Cusa solved an analogous problem by introducing axiomatic revolutionary change , namely circular action, a physical principle excluded from Euclidean

---

19. Leibniz, "The Ultimate Origin of Things," 1697, in **Leibniz: Selections**, (see footnote 10). "LaRouche's Discovery," (see footnote 2) page 39.

20. See footnote 2.

21. Lyndon LaRouche, "Leibniz from Riemann's Standpoint," **Fidelio**, Fall 1996. See "The Principle of Universal Characteristics" and the subsection on Riemann's Principle of Hypothesis. Also, Leibniz, "Towards

a Universal Characteristic" in **Leibniz: Selections**, page 17 (see footnote 10).

22. Lyndon LaRouche, **The Science of Christian Economy** (see footnote 16), see pages 258-259, 412, 419 and other references to the **Parmenides**. LaRouche there focuses on the problem of the one and the many.

geometry—which axiomatically only assumes lines and points—to subsume Archimedes' infinite series of inscribed and circumscribed polygons, with which Archimedes intended to trap the circle between, and thereby define its area. Cusa's discovery of the uniqueness of the circle, that it was of a different species and generating principle than the polygon, was the necessary predecessor for the discoveries of Kepler and Leonardo da Vinci, his acknowledged followers. Cusa's role in the Leibniz calculus will be cited later.[23]

Leibniz, a follower of Kepler, struggled for years with the "Labyrinth of the Continuum," so named because of its paradoxes pertaining to whether matter is continuous or not and whether it is infinitely divisible. This included Zeno's paradoxes of motion as well. Although Leibniz recognized that matter in principle—as is the clear case of a liquid—has no definite shape and is in constant flux. It is above all an infinite aggregate with no unifying principle that gives it an on-going identity.[24] At last, drawing on work by Huyghens in dynamics of elastic collisions, and his own redefinitions of the infinite and infinitesimal that led to his calculus, he was able to locate a singular intention in the behavior of matter expressed by a new physical principle, an innate power which he called live force or *vis viva* conserved in elastic collisions but, as distinct from Huyghens view, active in all collisions.[25] He was able to hypothesize a non-material *one*, the substantial form, which gave to associated matter its unity of action and continuing identity, and thereby governed the action of live force, which obeyed a universal physical principle, the conservation of live force. Today his live force, a principle of change, is stripped of its anti-entropic content and reduced to a thing, "kinetic energy." The substantial form was driven by an impulse or "appetition" to act, like all that is substantial, in Leibniz's view, i.e. the universe is alive down to its smallest part. Until his identification of this new principle of dynamics, which he later came to call the monad, the "substantial form" as named by previous philosophers, had been merely a tautology. It was therefore through *physics, not mathematics*, that Leibniz solved the labyrinth of the continuum, including Zeno's paradoxes. Living animals had the further distinction of being composed of machines down to their smallest part. Thus the organism as a whole, governed by its singular monad, was actually a hierarchy of subordinate monads. (This is what he called worlds within worlds.)[26] This was a prescient view considering there was as yet no microscopic observation of cells in tissues.

As previously described, LaRouche has taken this non-deductive process to a yet higher level, as applied to his study both of successive economic systems and the role of successive scientific discoveries and their incorporation into economic practice, social discourse and social organization in creating a society of increasing productivity and increasing energy flux density per capita. Again, knowledge or relative truth is to be found in the higher hypothesis that subsumes a series of such successive hypotheses or discoveries and their application via the machine tool principle in new technologies. The discovery of a new principle necessarily takes place in the mind of a sovereign human being or higher monad as an expression of freedom. LaRouche's discovery, which he made intelligible by basing it on his application of Riemannian physics to economy, re-

---

23. "LaRouche's Discovery," page 39 (see footnote 2). "Nicolaus's new solution for these [Archimedes theorems on trapping the circle between two converging sets of polygons-E.S.] is also a demonstration of the general solution for the ontological paradox depicted within Plato's **Parmenides** dialogue."

24. G.W. Leibniz, **The Labyrinth of the Continuum: Writings on the Continuum Problem, 1672-1686**, edited by Richard Arthur. The Yale Leibniz Series (Yale University Press, 2001). Arthur provides a lengthy introduction. See especially sections 6 and 7 of the Introduction by the translator and the translations he cites. For an understanding of how Leibniz arrived at his understanding of live force and the substantiality of the monad, these translations are essential. The translator's introduction and footnotes are very helpful. It was from a study of this material that I situated Leibniz's discovery as solution to the one-many problem. See also Leibniz, "New System of Nature and of the Communication of Substances as Well as of the Union of Body and Soul." (See footnote 10). See sections 1-4. See footnote, page 106, where Leibniz reviews his discovery of *vis viva* (live force) and shows how it was pivotal for all of his subsequent work in metaphysics.

25. , "Specimen Dynamicum" in Loemker, page 439. (See footnote 7.) "So far as I know, Huygens, whose brilliant discoveries have enlightened our age, was also the first to arrive at the pure and transparent truth in this matter, by formulating certain rules which were published long ago. Almost the same rules were obtained by Wren, Wallis, and Mariotte, all excellent men in this field, though in differing measure. But there is no unity of opinion about the causes. It would seem, indeed, that the true foundations of this science have not yet been revealed." Leibniz's non-inductive leap to live force and the metaphor of the monad was the founding of the science of dynamics. Unlike these other scientists, Leibniz discerned that a universal principle must be involved. That is why, unlike even Christiaan Huygens, he was not satisfied to account for elastic collisions, but insisted a solution must subsume inelastic collisions as well.

26. Nicholas Rescher, ed. **G.W. Leibniz's Monadology** (Pittsburgh: 1991). See sections 61-70. He develops the necessity for his worlds within worlds in the living animal, which implies the animal is a machine down to its smallest part, unlike a man-made machine.

solved the paradoxes that result when an economy is viewed from the reductionist standpoint of a notion of value based on ephemerals like money or labor content, in fact upon anything other than that which increases the rate of growth of productivity of the society as a totality.

To what extent did Leibniz share this theory of knowledge? I am not aware of any direct statement on his part. I think we are dealing with the limitations of historical specificity, because Leibniz was involved in only the very beginning of the industrial revolution with his science of dynamics and work on the first steam engine. However, LaRouche in his *LaRouche's Discovery* paper, in the course of the section "The Theory of Knowledge," asks the reader to concurrently study Leibniz's article of 1695: *A New System of Nature and of the Communication of Substances, as well as of the Union of Soul and Body*.[27] In this article, Leibniz presents his series of ground breaking discoveries in historical sequence beginning with the modern science of dynamics which he founded with his definition of live force. (Although he doesn't mention it there, his discovery of least action, elaborated in his joint work with Bernoulli on the catenary, has been essential for all of subsequent physics). He goes on to show how his notion of the substantial form, in turn led to new paradoxes, and he goes through his solutions in succession in the article, so he can in the end subsume them under his idea of pre-established harmony.

To summarize this section, it is the successive introduction of axiomatic revolutions in physical science, often made intelligible with the help revolutionary ideas in mathematics, that has led to human economic progress. This history needs to be taken as a whole to appreciate fully any particular discovery in the sequence, each discovery being replicated and reproduced in its historically specific form and context. LaRouche has emphasized that this approach to science education should supersede the textbook method, which deliberately leaves out the historical drama of conflicting and hotly debated higher hypotheses at stake in each of these cases cited.[28]

The Moral and Material Domains Together Under Natural Law: The Hypothesis of the Higher Hypothesis

As discussed in the introduction, LaRouche and Leibniz utilized their pivotal discoveries in physical economy and dynamics respectively to develop a system, an all-encompassing view of the universe and of human society acting upon and transforming itself through universal principles. By a system, I can best refer to LaRouche's section in **Dialectical Economics** on the phenomenological or dialectical method of proof.[29] Any particular, starting with the simplest and most pervasive phenomenon, can be understood only in its relationship with the ongoing *free* development of the totality. Situating the particular in any lesser domain leads to paradoxes. This coheres with the **Monadology**. Each monad, in Leibniz's words, has a perfect spontaneity, while its actions take into account everything else in the universe, based on God's design which tends towards progress. In his only full length book published in his lifetime,[30] **Theodicy**, Leibniz resolves the paradox of God's foreknowledge with man's free will, based on his distinction of contingent versus necessary truths and a principle of sufficient reason.[31]

Moreover for both Leibniz and LaRouche, the moral domain is multiply connected with the physical domain, by which I mean that every action we take has a particular significance in both domains, i.e. it is double valued.

---

27. **Leibniz: Selections**, page 106 cases cited (see footnote 10).

28. Lyndon LaRouche, "On the Subject of Education," discusses a classical education in science based on reliving the experience of successive discoveries. In "LaRouche's Discovery" (see footnote 2) he describes how this trains the student to find the ordering principle or higher hypothesis generating the series.

29. **Dialectical Economics**, pages 241-253. (See footnote 2.)

30. G.W. Leibniz, **Theodicy**. (Cosimo Classics, 2010). Part I, Essays on the Justice of God and the Freedom of Man in the Origin of Evil. See sections 279-300, especially section 300, discussing freedom as an aspect of pre-established harmony. See sections 58-66, addressing the relation of his metaphysics to the moral domain. See section 365 for the question of God's foreknowledge.

31. See sections 14 and 15 of the last part of the **Theodicy**, "Observations on the Book Concerning 'The origin of Evil' Recently published in London," for application of the principle of "sufficient reason," which he discusses in Leomker, "Leibniz On the General Characteristic ca. 1679" (see footnote 7), page 227. "This axiom, however, that there is nothing without a reason, must be considered one of the greatest and most fruitful of all human knowledge, for upon it is built a great part of metaphysics, physics, and moral science; without it, indeed the existence of God cannot be proved from his creatures, nor can an argument be carried from causes to effects or from effects to causes, nor any conclusions be drawn in civil matters. So true is this that whatever is not of mathematical necessity, as for instance are logical forms and numerical truths, must be sought here entirely." Regarding sufficient reason, see throughout the Leibniz-Clarke debate (see footnote 7), the hilarious, complete inability of Clarke-Newton to distinguish sufficient reason from arbitrary power.

For this reason, LaRouche supported and illustrated his voluntaristic definition of a universal physical principle by referring to the **Monadology**.[32] Such a principle is one we not only discover, but we then transmit it to others, and together we apply it to change the universe, which is predisposed to obey us. This coheres with Leibniz in the **Monadology,** saying God created the universe for spirits formed in his image, including us.

LaRouche saw in Leibniz's notion of the intention embedded in each monad, however lowly, the scientific basis for our own intention to transform the universe. What is implicit in Leibniz becomes apparent for man in the space age from LaRouche's standpoint. In yet another example of a principle of both the natural and moral domain, LaRouche extended Leibniz's dynamics to social processes such as the mass strike, where a powerful idea moves the population to act as a *one*. Such ideas may also be destructive ones. Percy Shelley portrays this principle of dynamics in the last paragraph of **A Defense of Poetry**.[33]

This LaRouche/Leibniz view of natural law removes the artificial separation of art, including statecraft, from science, a separation which has caused great harm to both. The creative quality of mind of the classical artist and statesman is expressed by metaphor in science as well. An education in re-experiencing the great discoveries in classical art and science is essential for the moral character, by focusing on that quality of creativity and freedom which distinguishes us from animals. The development of the modern nation state based on the common good in the 15th Century, represents a revolution in the application of the principles of natural law as a higher hypothesis.

The Calculus as Expression of a Higher Hypothesis

Does Leibniz's discovery of the differential calculus fit LaRouche's notion of progress through successive hypotheses of increasingly higher power? I believe it received an essential contribution from Cusa's idea of the Maximum-Minimum relationship.[34] Cusa wrote that in the Divine Mind, opposites such as the maximum and the minimum coincide, because the exemplars (forms) of all things are in God. In the actual physical world, however, this would imply that in any dynamic or living process acting as a one, what is essential about the whole, its intention, must be expressed in some way, even in its most infinitesimal part.

This maximum-minimum principle finds its leading expression in our relationship with the Creator in whose image we exist. As potentially creative beings, we share in His creativity and are in a direct unmediated relationship with Him. Thus, in a section of the **Science of Christian Economy** entitled "Leibniz's Mind," LaRouche elaborates the implications of the fact that "the organization of the universe is based on the action corresponding to creative reason by monads." Later, "that gives us the essential map of the universe in germ." Later still, "Hence, the **Monadology** is perhaps the most essential document in all of physics."

LaRouche continues: "You will note that Leibniz, in essence, says in his own terms of reference, exactly what I say here—which is not entirely incidental; about the age of 13 or14, I learned this from Leibniz directly. I wrestled with it then for over a year and I got it into my head; so, today, I don't have it necessarily in the form I learned it from Leibniz, although I was stimulated to my discovery by him."

Kepler, a follower of Cusa, applied Cusa's insight to finding a knowable relationship between an infinitesimal portion of the planetary orbit and the orbit taken as a totality.[35] According to his area law, the area swept

---

32. **Economics of the Noösphere** (see footnote 1), section "Monadology," starting page 126.

33. LaRouche elaborates his view of dynamics in "Economics as History," (see footnote 18) as a conception applying to both the social domain and to physical science.

34. Nicholas of Cusa, **On Learned Ignorance**, Jasper Hopkins, tr.

(A.J. Banning Press, 1985). In Book II, Chapter 9, Cusa uses his maximum-minimum principle to show that the Platonic and Aristotelian views of the exemplars—forms (of things are necessarily incorrect. Thus the Platonists situate forms in a world soul. Cusa agrees with the Platonists that the intelligence that directs change must be based on exemplars or forms, contrary to the Peripatetics, including Aristotle, but to situate pure uncontracted possibility, i.e. a maximum, anywhere but in God violates the maximum-minimum principle. Being therefore both in God, maximum and minimum must coincide. See online pedagogical **Riemann for Antidummies** number 59, "Think Infinitesimal," by Bruce Director for elaboration of Cusa's contribution to development of calculus and modern science. Bruce Director's pedagogical series, especially the many numbers which elaborate the history of the complex domain and its application to mapping by Gauss and Riemann, demonstrates the application of an ordering principle or higher hypothesis in great depth, especially by showing the necessary connection of modern science with principles discovered by the ancient Greeks. They are available on the Internet.

35. Johannes Kepler, **Astronomia Nova**, translated by William A. Donahue (Santa Fe: Green Lion Press, 2015). See chapters 40 and 59.

out, taking the orbit as an ellipse with the Sun at one focus, is proportional always to the time. This implies a determined relation between the total orbit and any portion of it, and further, since each orbit is different, the possibility of harmonic relationships between the orbits of different planets exists. Kepler recognized that his area law still did not allow one to precisely calculate where the planet would be at a given subsequent time, so he challenged future mathematicians to solve this problem.[36]

Leibniz studied Kepler's work extensively, especially after he found Newton's explanation of universal gravitation unacceptable. Leibniz sought a way to account for Kepler's results based on true universal physical principles rather than occult action at a distance, which contradicted Leibniz's view that force must be transmitted through a form of contact. Above all, Newton's system violated Leibniz's principle of pre-established harmony, since it implied a direct action of one substance on another substance.[37]

Although he could not solve the Kepler problem mentioned above, Leibniz through his differential calculus was able to represent how the physical principle generating a total trajectory can be used to define the intention of the process at any given interval, however

Johannes Kepler (1571-1630)

small.[38] By using his method of differentials, he was able to express its nonlinear characteristic, based upon insights gained in his struggle with the Labyrinth of the Continuum. In particular, he concluded that there are no true infinitesimals. Rather, they are fictions to be used by us voluntaristically. That allowed him, where appropriate, to assert that a numerical magnitude could be made as small as we wished.[39]

Leibniz's calculus exemplified a principle LaRouche has taken to a higher level, metaphor, by developing its fundamental role in both scientific discovery and artistic creation. Humorless critics of Leibniz's calculus, such as Richard Courant, insisted on taking Leibniz's

---

36. Bruce Director and Jonathan Tennenbaum, "How Gauss Determined the Orbit of Ceres, **Fidelio**, Summer 1998. See page 25, "Kepler Calls for a New Geometry," for an in depth study of what is called the "Kepler problem."

37. Paolo Bussotti, **The Complex Itinerary of Leibniz's Planetary Theory** (Birkhäuser Publishers, 2015). See especially page 152 regarding action at a distance. In the case of an elastic collision, Leibniz saw the recoil as resulting from the activation of the innate or potential force in each body. This accords with his Platonic notion of innate ideas which are latent and potential in our mind, but which only come to awareness when we reflect upon experiences. Analogously, LaRouche also identifies the unique role of metaphor to provoke a thought object in the mind of the listener. Leibniz criticized Kepler for hypothesizing magnets in the Sun and planets to account for their interaction, in "Against Barbaric Physics," in **G.W. Leibniz: Philosophical Essays**, translated by Roger Ariew and Daniel Garber (1989).

38. Ernest Schapiro, "The Real Calculus versus What You Learned" (see footnote 17).

39. Refer to footnote 24. See page 65, "On the Infinitely Small," regarding infinitesimals as useful fictions, and relevant footnotes; see pages 393-4, 396 . See page 89 of "Infinite Numbers" for discussion of the circle as a fiction. In **The Secrets of the Sublime, Labyrinth of the Continuum**, page 49, he says if "matter is actually divided into an infinity of points ... hence it follows further that any part of matter is commensurable with any other. ... In that connection, I should examine the line of reasoning I have used elsewhere, according to what it seems to follow that a circle, if it exists, has a ratio to the diameter of one number to another ... Hence it follows that any part of matter is commensurable with any other." Leibniz is saying that were there to be actual infinitesimals, the circle could be squared. Instead, there are no actual infinitesimals; they, like the circle, are useful fictions. In fact, "the ideal determines the real." This last quote is from Letter to Varignon, with a note on the "Justification of the Infinitesimal Calculus by that of Ordinary Algebra." Loemker, pages 542-546. Leibniz arrived at this revolutionary view of infinitesimals in 1676 in Paris, the same year he concluded that in finding the area under a curve by integration, one need not divide the base below the curve into equal infinitesimal units, but simply can take the subdivisions as small as one liked. I believe he was the first to take this bold step. See **The Early Mathematical Manuscripts of Leibniz,** translated by J.M. Child (Open Court Publishers, 1920), page 125. See pages 183-187 in **Labyrinth of the Continuum**, "Dialogue on Continuity and Motion," for his critique of Descartes on infinite divisibility of liquids, and hence of matter generally (see footnote 24). Leibniz's argument against actual infinitesimals involves mathematics *and* physics, because both are subsumed under metaphysics. Richard Arthur's introduction (pages li-lxi) is an insightful review of the evolution of Leibniz's views of the infinitesimal.

dy/dx literally, arguing that it implies dividing by zero at the point where dy/dx is being evaluated. LaRouche sees metaphor—in sciences and in classical art—as a means of pointing to an elaborated invisible principle, what he calls a thought object,[40] e.g. Leibniz's monad or Riemann's *geistesmassen*,[41] which represents the solution to a paradox not solvable by deductive methods. By means of the metaphor, the original idea can be evoked, not by "information" but rather by a creative mental effort that replicates the thought object The thought object for dy/dx subsumes the process by which Leibniz resolved paradoxes of the infinitely small and infinitely large. It also represents the interaction of an invisible principle with the trajectory.[42]

By historically situating Leibniz's discovery of calculus as one of a series of fundamental breakthroughs, including those of Cusa and Kepler, Leibniz's and Bernoulli's joint elaboration of the calculus in physical "least action," and Gauss's later application of calculus to mapping the complex domain, a lot has been gained. The grasp of metaphysics and of the method of hypothesis common to each of them makes clear why Newton, who crassly asserted: "I don't make hypotheses," could not possibly have independently developed calculus. It also helps us understand why so much effort up to the present day, has gone into obfuscating Leibniz's method of hypothesis, and ignoring the importance of his many years of struggle with the "labyrinth of the continuum."

LaRouche also utilized Cusa's maximum-minimum principle underlying the calculus as a higher hypothesis in his 1980's seminar discussions with scientists including Dr. Daniel R. Wells and Dr. Robert Moon, who had hypothesized a quantized structure for physical space time, and, by implication' for the atomic nucleus itself. In response, LaRouche proposed that the atomic nucleus must be Keplerian, as the minimum, in reciprocal relationship to the Solar system as the maximum. LaRouche has referred to this as the "reciprocity of extremes."[43] Moon proceeded to devise a model of

nested platonic solids, which corresponded to and predicted many facts of atomic physics and important features of the Periodic Table.[44]

Calculus, In Turn, Generates a New, Higher Hypothesis, Least Action

As an outgrowth of his calculus and his principle of sufficient reason, Leibniz was able to more rigorously define unique action, i.e. that path of action which could be achieved in only one way. He applied that to the reflection and refraction of light,[45] and together with Bernoulli, to the shape of the catenary.[46] Leibniz's insight involved his principle of sufficient reason. Therefore when it comes to the path of reflection from a mirror, the universe will select the path whose length can be achieved in only one way. All other possible path lengths occur as "twins" and there is no basis for

<hr>

radiation necessarily tells us about the universe as a whole, and how it might express the interaction of principles.

44. Numerous articles since 1987 on the Moon model of the atomic nucleus in **EIR** and **21st Century Science & Technology** are available on the Internet.

45. Leibniz, "Tentamen Anagogicum, An Anagogical Essay on the Investigation of Causes," in Loemker (see footnote 7), page 477.

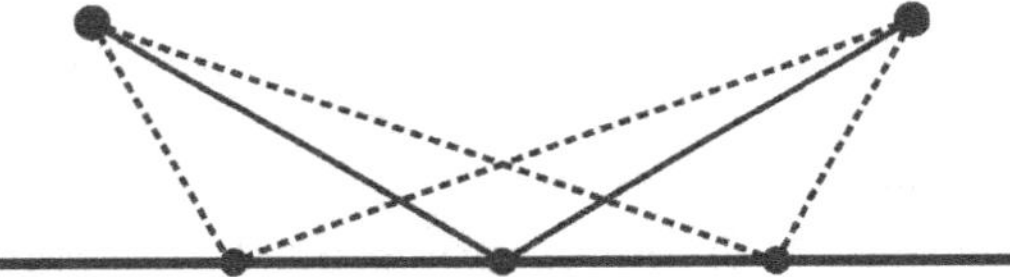

In both the cases of reflection and refraction, he obtained what he called the "most determined magnitude" by using his calculus to find the maximum or minimum of the path length or time taken, respectively. In the simpler case of reflection, where the least action path is the total path length from emitter to absorber by way of the mirror, he argues that with one exception, any particular path length can be achieved in two ways; i.e., there are two equal, total path lengths resulting from two points of reflection on the mirror. The exception is the unique total path length, whereby the twin points of reflection coalesce. That unique point lies between the twin points for all of the pairs. See Leibniz's diagram and explanation on page 480. A further geometric representation is in Richard Courant and Herbert Robbins, **What Is Mathematics**, (Oxford University Press, 1978), page 330.

46. Johann Bernoulli, "Lectures on the Integral Calculus," translated by William A. Ferguson, **21st Century Science & Technology**, Spring 2004. Here the least action form of the hanging chain was achieved by basing the mathematical formulation upon the physical assumption that every portion of the chain, however small, includes the original lowest point, satisfies the same set of conditions. That ensured that all such chains are still catenaries and fulfills Leibniz's broader conception of what came to be called "least action."

<hr>

40. "LaRouche On the Subject of Metaphor," Fidelio Fall, 1992.

41. **Bernhard Riemann: Philosophical Fragments, "section 1. On Psychology and Metaphysics**," in **21st Century Science & Technology**, Winter 1995-1996. Or Helga Zepp-LaRouche, "Overcoming Your Fears by Increasing Your Geistesmassen," **EIR**, Oct. 10, 2003.

42. Bruce Director, "Think Infinitesimal," **Riemann for Anti-Dummies** Number 59, addresses Leibniz's calculus in depth, using animations to illuminate the relation of a trajectory to unseen principles.

43. Lyndon LaRouche, "The Reciprocity of Extremes: The Astrophysics of Gurwitsch Radiation," in **21st Century Science & Technology**, Fall 1998. Here LaRouche asks what the phenomenon of mitogenetic

choice—see drawing. That unique path in this case is also the shortest. Leibniz's discovery was subsequently applied to the dynamics of moving bodies as "least action," action having the dimension of *energy times time* for a particular path.

Least action as conceived more generally by Leibniz, was a Platonic idea or thought object expressing a universal physical principle that itself qualifies as a leading example of a higher hypothesis which has generated in turn an ongoing series of discoveries, starting with Cusa's discovery and application of the fact that circular action uniquely generates that closed perimeter which encloses the maximum possible area, i.e. it constitutes a path of action achievable in only one way, which is an important aspect of what Leibniz meant by what came to be called "least action."

Kepler took Cusa's idea of "unique action" further by utilizing the sphere, instead of the circle, as primary. He took the nested five Platonic solids uniquely resulting from equal partitioning of the surface of the sphere by great circles as representing the orbits of the known six planets.[47] He later developed the idea of elliptical planetary orbits, i.e. conic sections,[48] anticipating by nearly 200 years the higher form of unique action developed by Gauss's discovery of the complex domain. In this reference,[49] Gauss shows that a complex number is equivalent to a combination of linear extension and rotational action. LaRouche elaborated Gauss's complex domain, making it intelligible as the continuous domain of conic self similar spiral least action.[50]

Carl Friedrich Gauss

By implication, the elliptical planetary orbits are self-similar spiral paths around a cone. Further, in defining the musical harmonic relationships among the elliptical planetary orbits by their relative angular velocities as viewed from the Sun, Kepler was modeling the Solar system on a metaphorical musical or aesthetic archetype, emanating from the mind of the Creator without reference to forces.[51]

In the view of LaRouche, this was an expression of force-free action or least action obeying the curvature of physical space time. LaRouche is the first in recent times to relate the musical scale to the principles of astrophysics. By thus identifying the musical scale with a universal physical principle, LaRouche's historic rediscovery has clarified the coherence between the necessary tuning of the musical scale and the biological properties of the trained force-free human singing voice, upon which the classical tradition from Bach to Brahms was based.

It was Leibniz, a follower of Kepler, who made unique action part of the broader conception underlying his universal pre-established harmony, going beyond a purely mathematical-physical conception to its being an expression of the fitness of things. In an essay, previously cited on how final causes are required to understand why physical laws take their particular form, Leibniz points out, in the cases of reflection and refraction of light as examples:

"The most beautiful thing about this new view [of God's work—E. Schapiro] seems to me to be that the property of perfection is not limited to the general but

---

47. Johannes Kepler, **Mysterium Cosmographicum** (1596), facsimile of the original Latin of the second edition of 1621, translated by A.M. Duncan (Abaris Books, 1981).

48. Johannes Kepler, **New Astronomy** (1609), translated by William H. Donahue (Cambridge University Press, 1993).

49. Karl Gauss, "The Metaphysics of Complex Numbers," translated by Jonathan Tennenbaum, **21st Century Science & Technology**, Spring 1990.

50. This video on The Power of Labor from the early 1980's introduces LaRouche's view of conical action as an expression of action in the complex domain. It also makes possible the distinction between work and energy. The complex domain plays a central role in LaRouche's work as the domain of universal physical principles or the domain of powers and of possibility. Plato's metaphor of the cave portrays the relationship of this higher domain to the world of our perceptions. PPSee also Chapter 3 of LaRouche. So, You Wish to Learn All About Economics? (Washington: EIR News Service, 1995). PPLaRouche, "Visualizing the Complex Domain," . Because the complex domain typifies what makes us human, i.e. our power to hypothesize the universal principles giving rise to perceptions, LaRouche demonstrates the grievous immorality of those like Leonhard Euler and Augustan-Louis Cauchy, who would reduce the complex domain to a mathematical device.

51. Kepler, **The Harmony of the World**, translated by A.J. Aiton, et al. (American Philosophical Society, 1997).

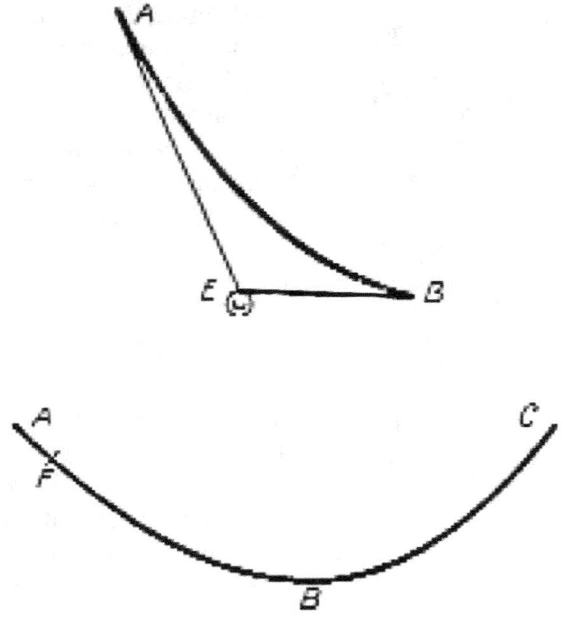

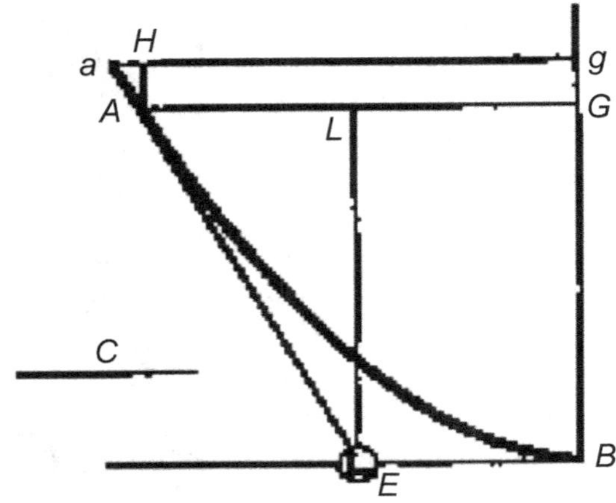

As we change the point of suspension from A to F, the shape of the remaining portion remains the same. The smaller catenary thus retains the same optimal characteristic as the original.

descends to the particulars of things and of phenomena, and that in this respect it closely resembles the method of optimal forms, i.e. forms that provide a maximum or minimum as the case may be—a method which I introduced into geometry in addition to the ancient method of maximum and minimal quantities. For in these forms or figures, the optimum is found not only in the whole but also in the part, and it would not even suffice in the whole without this.

How does the catenary conform to Leibniz's optimal form, as demonstrated above? It takes the unique shape that minimizes the work required to elevate it to where it is suspended from its particular endpoints, and therefore, conversely, the energy acquired in its falling to the ground. Also, if in **(Figure 1)** (see reference by Bernoulli), one changes the point of suspension from A to F, the shape of the remaining portion remains the same, and the horizontal force remains the same. The smaller catenary thus retains the same optimal characteristic as the original of which it was a part. Supposing the vertical direction is y and the horizontal is x, the slope of the tangent at any point along the chain, i.e., the ratio of the vertical and horizontal sides of the infinitesimal triangle, aHA in Figure 2, can be understood by Bernoulli's astute physical reasoning, because it is at the same time the ratio of the weight of the chain below

the point at which we are taking the tangent, that is to say, the vertical force, to the horizontal force. The horizontal force is a constant throughout the length of the chain, including even the lowest point, where there is no vertical force. It is the changing value of this ratio that ensures the stability and gracefulness of the hanging chain **(Figure 2)**. Leibniz's invention of the calculus allowed him and Bernoulli to calculate the relevant length of the curved chain and invert its rate of change, dy/dx, i.e. integrate, thereby bringing to the surface the invisible process underlying the rate of change, which is to determine the hidden form of the entire catenary, as actually the arithmetic mean of two exponential curves.

However this physical least action is only the beginning, leading on to *cognitive* least action.[52] He describes that as follows:

> As for the simplicity of the ways of God, this is shown especially in the means which he uses, whereas the variety, opulence, and abundance appears in regard to the ends or results . It is true that nothing costs God anything less than it costs

---

52. For a helpful portrayal of cognitive least action, see Bruce Director, **Riemann for Anti-Dummies** number 37 "The Domain of Possibility" and number 40, "Cognitive Least Action." Director reveals the harmony introduced among the exponential and trigonometric functions and the conic sections made possible by the discovery of the complex domain by Gauss and Riemann.

a philosopher to build the fabric of his imaginary world out of hypotheses, since God has only to make his decrees in order in order to create a real world. But where wisdom is concerned, decrees or hypotheses are comparable to expenditures, in the degree to which they are independent of each other, for reason demands that we avoid multiplying hypotheses or principles, somewhat as the simplest system is always preferred in astronomy.[53]

In his first article in 1691 on the catenary, he writes:

The resourcefulness of this curve is only equal to the simplicity of its construction, which makes it the primary one among all of the transcendental curves [curves generated by motion-E. Schapiro]. …The curve can be constructed and traced very simply by a physical type of construction, that is, by suspending a string, or better a small chain of variable length, and as soon as you can discover its curve, you can discover all of the proportional means, and all of the logarithms that you want to find, as well as the quadrature ofhe hyperbola [the area under a section of the hyperbola—E.S.].[54]

But Leibniz's own discoveries were not the last expression of the opulence of the catenary. In solving the form of the curve, one encounters the sine, the hyperbola, and the actual form of the curve, the arithmetic mean of two exponential curves. Leibniz asked: What higher domain could subsume all of these transcendental functions? Also, what power could generate powers of negative numbers, such as the square root of minus 1, i.e. what was its logarithm? It was Gauss who answered Leibniz's questions by discovering the physical complex domain in which these functions could all be represented intelligibly in terms of the complex exponential function.[55] In so doing, Gauss refuted Euler, who treated the "imaginary numbers" as merely a useful formalism. Again, it was LaRouche who made an explicit

representation of Gauss's idea in three dimensions as conical self similar spiral action, a higher form of least action than simple circular action.[56]

LaRouche has advanced the representation of still higher forms of unique action, this time capable of generating physical, not just mathematical, singularities, as well as explicitly developing the conception of unique action as force free. The higher forms he proposed involved not one single cone but a cone whose apex angle keeps expanding as it grows in time, so that one gets a hyperbolic cone that flares out to infinity. A succession of such flaring cones thus yields a series of singularities.

The Leibnizian principle of unique action has been reapplied throughout subsequent history. The most notable example might be its use by William Hamilton to develop a metaphor subsuming particle trajectory in mechanics with light pathway in geometrical optics. Erwin Schrödinger a century later utilized this largely overlooked metaphor to develop wave mechanics. Most recently, Vladimir Vernadsky's three laws of the biosphere are based on an optimizing principle.[57] It must not be forgotten that Leibniz saw "unique action" as an expression of natural law and natural theology. God selects that universe which, taken as a whole, has from His standpoint the least imperfection and also the greatest potential for further perfection and beauty. This principle has found so many different historically specific expressions that only by seeing the entire sequence can we do it justice and arrive at a higher conception subsuming them all. Thus, an important area of inquiry where such a review of least action is relevant is the millennium-long debate of the relative significance of negentropic potential as opposed to force in all three domains: the inorganic, living processes, and cognitive processes.

Can Unique Action Processes Be Force-Free?

As regards force-free pathways, LaRouche was convinced from an early point in his development that

---

53. Leibniz, "Discourse on Metaphysics." See Loemker (footnote 7), page 306.
54. Leibniz, "Two Papers on the Catenary Curve and the Logarithmic Curve, 1691," translated by Pierre Beaudry, **Fidelio**, Spring 2001. By "logarithmic" Leibniz means exponential.
55. Bruce Director, **Riemann for Antidummies**, number 49. "The Hidden History of the Complex Domain."

56. See footnote 50.
57. Andrey Lapo, **Traces of Bygone Biospheres** (copublished by Mir Publishing, Moscow, and Synergetic Press, Inc., Oracle, Arizona and London, 1987.

the planetary orbits harmoniously express the physical curvature of space time. Similarly, as opposed to the Newtonian view of forces acting at a distance through empty space to keep them in place, Leibniz proposed that the planets are surrounded by rotating ethereal vortices which cause all the planets to circulate in the same direction and also exert a net inward pressure opposing the planet's tendency to fly off on the tangent. He also suggested the possible role of the Sun radially emitting a material cause for gravitational attraction falling off as the square of the distance.[58]

LaRouche had force free processes in mind at a seminar in 1985. There he offered a suggestion to a plasma physicist, Dr. Daniel Wells, who was working on fusion energy from a plasma confined with the help of a magnetic field. Wells had invented a device called Trisops which projected plasma braided rings—composed of vortex filaments—from opposite ends of an enclosure and sought to prolong their stable lifetime in a magnetic field long enough for fusion to occur. LaRouche asked Wells if he had he applied his concept of plasma vortices stabilized in a magnetic field by balanced opposing forces to the formation of the Solar system. Wells had never seriously considered the problem until then! Wells' solution to LaRouche's challenging question started with cylindrical concentric rings of plasma in a magnetic field which eventually shrank down to braided tori—called Beltrami vortices—such as he observed in his machine. These rings in turn would each suddenly condense into a single ball, which he called the White Owl phenomenon. His calculation varied the parameters governing the relative amount of two opposing forces so as to equalize them, as well as minimizing the free energy of the system. The two opposing forces were: (1) a mechanical interaction between the plasma and the vortices rotating in it, known as the Magnus force, i.e., the force that lifts an airplane in flight; (2) An opposing force, due to the interaction of the magnetic field with the moving electric charges in the rotating rings, called the Lorentz force. By setting these opposing forces equal to one another, he obtained a remarkable result, using the calculus. The solutions to the variational problem were very close to the known planetary orbits in their relative velocities and relative distances from the Sun. They were also consistent with the varying magnetic properties of the individual planets.

In the conclusion to the article in which he reported these results, he said:

> We have obtained the geometry of the rings— planets—and the velocity ratios with a three dimensional field theory that is independent of any "action at a distance" forces, that is, is independent of gravitation. We have asked, what would the distances and velocities of the planets have to be if they were to achieve stable—that is, force-free—orbits, and all have orbital rotation in the same direction?

After describing the method of calculation, he continued:

> We discovered that the [observed—E.S.] Bode numbers for the inner planets are actually eigenvalues (roots) of the force-free field equation.

With a knowledge of the initial conditions of the system, obviously not known to us, "then a detailed description of both the morphology and scale of the system would be determined without invoking the gravitational inverse square law.

"This was the objective of Kepler, who took the opposite approach to that of Newton and Galileo. He did not view 'forces' as primary; instead, he derived his laws of planetary motion from the physical geometry of the planets and the Sun."[59]

LaRouche saw this as a major contribution to theoretical physics, because it offered a force-free account of planetary motion and of a particular many-body problem. Many-body problems are not solvable by purely mathematical methods; the only solution thus far has been Kepler's use of the modulated "hard and soft musical scales" to account for the planetary system as a whole, including the multiply-connected interaction of the planets with the Sun and with one another.[60]

---

58. Paolo Bussotti (see footnote 37). He not only develops Leibniz's work on planetary motion, but clarifies the influence of Kepler's method on Leibniz's own thinking. Leibniz used his calculus to intelligibly account for elliptical orbits and took Kepler's ideas of astrophysical harmony to a higher level in his monadology based on pre-established harmony.

59. Daniel R. Wells, "How the Solar System Was Formed," **21st Century Science & Technology**, July-August 1988, page 18.
60. LaRouche Memo of April 11, 1986: "The Coming Report on Kep-

Therefore, in a sense, Kepler's musical exemplar and metaphor is a still higher and more beautiful conception, than Wells's "physical geometry of the planets and the Sun." That is the case because Kepler expresses the curvature of physical space time. It is likely to have contributed to Leibniz's arriving at his pre established harmony. Again, Kepler was the first to identify the musical scale with fundamental principles of astrophysics. LaRouche has given this discovery new significance by rediscovering that the proper tuning of the scale must conform to the biophysics of the human singing voice. Tuning, therefore, which has in recent decades been treated as an arbitrary matter of taste is therefore a scientific question. Arbitrary tunings which raise the pitch strain and ultimately injure the vocal apparatus.[61]

The distinction between dynamis, Plato's principle of powers, such as the cognitive power by which we double a square; and Aristotle's notion of force as a self-evident push or pull, is the precursor of bitter and repeated scientific controversy. Kepler saw the planetary motions as a dynamic totality fulfilling an idea or intention guided harmoniously by the Sun, whereas Newton saw only pairwise forceful interactions using a

Bernhard Riemann

formula plagiarized from Kepler's third law.[62]

Leibniz' focus of attack on Newton in the Leibniz-Clarke debate was Newton's oligarchical view that God acted arbitrarily and ruled by force, whereas his own God acted on the basis of creative reason—which he also called "necessary and sufficient reason." In his book-length critique of John Locke, in which Leibniz saw our most fundamental ideas as innate, Locke's associate argued that ideas are in effect inserted into the mind, comparing it to a passive blank slate.[63]

One hundred years later, the elaboration of a potential function by Karl Friedrich Gauss and Bernhard Riemann, and its essential role in their electromagnetic theories, starting with André-Marie Ampère's force free experiments, contrasts with Maxwell's elaboration of Michael Faraday's force fields. Riemann was one of the first to propose that electromagnetic waves represent propagation of a potential, an invisible thought object, with the speed of light, whereas Maxwell rejected the idea of potential as, at most, a mathematical construct. The development of the metaphor of the complex domain by Gauss and Riemann enabled them to conceive of a new domain of physical powers manifested as least-action pathways of increasing complexity, such as elliptical orbits.

LaRouche's proposal to Wells was an intervention into this historic debate against the unjustified authority of Newtonian methods in physics assuming the primacy of self-evident forces, which LaRouche encountered even among his closest collaborators in the scientific community. Historically, the idea of potential has

---

lerian Orbits" in Local Plasma and Related Events. LaRouche elaborates the revolutionary implications of the work of plasma physicist Daniel Wells supporting Kepler's relatively force free model of the solar system as opposed to that of Newton. The orbits and their harmonic proportions, as developed by Kepler in **Harmony of the World**, reflect the natural curvature of physical space time, and the musical scale appropriate to the human singing voice. An interesting question concerns why it should be that, by minimizing the free energy and force in a magnetohydrodynamic model of the plasma of the early solar system, one not only derives the known planetary orbits, but also approximates the musical scale which Kepler derived using the relative angular velocities of rotation of the planets around the Sun. There must be a principle applicable to both the biophysics of the singing and speaking voice and to planetary motion, i.e. what LaRouche called at that time a strong hypothesis.

61. A Manual on the Rudiments of Tuning and Registration, "Book I, Introduction and Human Singing Voice," (Schiller Institute, 1992).

---

62. **Science of Christian Economy** (see footnote 16), pages 374-376, "How Newton Parodied Kepler's Discovery," gives the details of the bowdlerization of Kepler's Third Law. The greater crime, however, was to conceptually reduce a principle of the Solar system as a whole to a so called law of pairwise interaction.

63. Leibniz: **New Essays on Human Understanding**, translated by Peter Remnant and Jonathan Bennett (Cambridge University Press, 1982).

been the means of elaborating a principle of anti-entropy and unlimited progress.

The Monadology Expresses a Pervasive Principle of Intention in the Universe

LaRouche sees the **Monadology** as Leibniz's greatest contribution to physics, and his discovery of least action as leading directly to his **Monadology**. My interpretation of this latter statement is that the **Monadology**, an elaboration of Leibniz's pre-established harmony, is the way the universe must be organized for least action to be possible. Least action, then, would be the entire universe expressing a universal physical principle by acting as a *one* to effect a result. LaRouche applied that idea to astrophysical processes which involve spatial order over such vast distances that one might hypothesize that the organizing intention must be conveyed at speeds far greater than light, in what he called "absolute time."[64] He also cited the case of a scientist who takes the discovery of someone from hundreds of years ago to a higher level. In that case he has instantaneously changed the significance of the original discovery. Raphael's painting *The School of Athens* might be a metaphor for that experience which LaRouche calls the "simultaneity of eternity." Convergent evolution, in which a form present in the past, such as feathers in reptiles, recurs in a much higher form of life—birds in this case—can represent an intention that has been preserved in some fashion so that it can act once again across millions of years.[65]

LaRouche is unique in his application of the role of intention in all possible domains, by showing that universal physical principles actually constitute intention. When we discover and as a society apply them, we change the universe. In his essay "The Gravity of Economic Intentions,"[66] where he discusses "truly knowing Leibniz's calculus," he emphasizes the disastrous implications for today's economists that the reduction of Leibniz's calculus to a mathematical technique, premised on linearity in the small, has had. The economist who sees economic cycles in monetary terms is at a loss to answer the question: What must we do now, in the small, to alter for the better the larger course of an economic cycle?

We must introduce a new physical principle, expressed via a technology, to change the productivity of the economy as a whole. A good example was Kennedy's introduction of a crash space program, and the inverse, the destructive effects on the entire economy of Obama's termination of the manned space program. Unfortunately, an economy is usually seen as the sum of millions of percussive interactions, lacking an intention, i.e., a self organizing principle, and therefore a foreseeable outcome. A shock wave, which is ordinarily also seen as an aggregate of percussive interactions, is described by LaRouche as actually a self-organized hydrodynamic process.[67] He has treated the form of Riemann's discovery of the shock wave as a universal phenomenon and written at length about economic shock waves.

---

64. A 1988 memo by Lyndon LaRouche: "A Non-Mystical View of the Necessity of Existence of the Notion of 'Absolute Time.'" See chapter 16.

65. Martin Lockley, **The Eternal Trail**, (Reading, Mass.: Perseus Books, 1999). He makes several references to his belief in a morphogenetic field, to account for the reappearance of similar harmonic patterns of body organization at vast time intervals as the remarkable phenomenon of convergent evolution. He also shows how the succession in time of morphologies itself constitutes a gestalt that gets repeated at vastly separated time intervals. See the chapter Spirit Trails, where he says: "One might describe it as evolution spiraling around a cone, so that each cycle resonates with the forms that manifest at that point in the cycle." This view is somewhat parallel with Rupert Sheldrake's controversial hypothesis on morphic resonance, which postulates a type of "field" or growth habit which influences successive generations to grow into similar shapes. I arrived independently at the conclusion that this view has merit through the study of fossil vertebrates and their tracks in the dimension of evolutionary time."

66. Lyndon LaRouche, **The Economics of the Noösphere** (see footnote 1). The idea is also elaborated in LaRouche, "Economics: The End of a Delusion." See the section "The Physical Basis of Economic Cycles" where he says: "The motion within any local, much shorter interval, must be understood as an expression of the orbit as a whole; not, contrary to today's typically foolish Wall Street statistician, the orbit as an expression of the cumulative effect of localized motions. This is as true for economic cycles, as it is for Solar ones. This approach to the principle of cycles, was, incidentally, the method underlying and permeating the original, 1676, first published announcement of the calculus by Gottfried Leibniz; therefore, the principle I am invoking here, is by no means a Johnny-come-lately innovation, but is an elemenetary and solid matter of scientific method, as should be taught in all respectable secondary schools and universities today."

67. "What Are Economic Shock Waves?" See two *EIR* articles, Dec. 7, 1982, and Dec. 14, 1982. PPThey were written with the expectation that the SDI would be adopted by the Reagan Administration and the then-Soviet Union, and therefor that once the SDI's new physical principles were incorporated into the civilian economies, there would be an economic shock wave.

An Autobiographical Note: Why the Theme of this Article?

I proposed to do a class series around the theme of Leibniz from LaRouche's Standpoint because in the months before, I had been asked—in early 2015—to do a Leibniz class series with Phil Rubinstein. I had benefitted personally from LaRouche's idea of looking at any given discovery as one member of a historically specific series of discoveries, and then seeking the subsuming higher hypothesis.

In particular, I had become intrigued by the question of formative causation, i.e., are there immaterial exemplars which, while exerting little or no force, are able to guide, i.e. inform the processes of morphogenesis in molecular processes, morphogenesis in biology, and mental processes? In the 1980's, our organization began to research and feature the work of Alexander Gurwitsch who was able to histologically diagram the successive stages of development of embryos. He then showed that he could superpose a vectorial field at each stage predicting the ensuing change in geometry of the cells and their layers, including the direction of orientation of the cell nuclei. He characterized this as a nonmaterial, non-energetic field, something never previously described, which he called the "dynamic preformed morpha."[68]

In 2012 I discovered the work of Rupert Sheldrake, including his book **The New Science of Life**. He generalized Gurwitsch's idea, but in the broadest, non-specific terms, to a much wider range of phenomena, including both non-living and cognitive.[69]

However, Sheldrake is extremely controversial, so I had at that time nothing to compare him with until after reading "Riemann Refutes Euler,"[70] by LaRouche, I read one of his references, "Riemann's Philosophical Fragments," translated in the same issue, wherein Riemann proposes that the mind of the earth or biosphere takes into itself the thought masses (Geistesmassen) of deceased plants and uses them (perhaps as an exemplar) to produce new species of plants. This seemed to be compatible with Sheldrake.

However, it was only after reading LaRouche's essay "Changing the Universe, a Philosophy of Victory," where he discussed historical specificity in relation to his theory of knowledge as higher hypothesis, it occurred to me I needed to do a much wider search for the idea of formative causation in a series of historically specific locations. I readily found the idea of formative causation elaborated in Cusa, Kepler, and above all in its first proponent, Plato. In the first section of **Parmenides**, it is the subject of heated debate between the young Socrates and Parmenides. Cusa made numerous references to formative causation.

> However because all living things have a natural understanding, a firm recollection, of their sustenance, and a sense of their similitude, and sense which beings are of the same species, Plato says this must necessarily stem from the idea, since nothing endures except ideas. From this you elicit that the ideas are thus not separated from individuals, as if they were extrinsic exemplars. For the nature of the individual is united with the idea, from which it has everything in a natural manner.

He is saying that something akin to mind is acting causally but not necessarily in the way we would ordinarily think of mind acting.

> Proclus explains more fully how the essential principles are intrinsic and not extrinsic, and how the individual by means of that contact in which the individual is joined to its idea, is connected through this intelligible idea to the divinity, so that according to its capacity it exists in the best manner in which it can be and be preserved.[71]

Kepler in his discussion of the ability of animals and humans to discern harmony in music says:

> For to recognize is to compare some external sensible thing with ideas which are internal, and to judge that they are congruent. That is splen-

---

68. Michael Lipkind, Alexander Gurwitsch, "The Concept of the Biological Field," **21st Century Science & Technology**, Summer 1998, Part 1; and Fall 1998 Part 2 . Both issues also feature LaRouche's in depth view of Gurwitsch's work.

69. See footnote 66.

70. See footnote 18.

71. Nicolaus of Cusa, **Toward a New Council of Florence: On the Peace of Faith and Other Works by Nicolaus of Cusa,** edited by Marinna Wertz (Washington: Schiller Institute, 1993). In this volume, see Cusa, "The Hunt for Wisdom," pages 462-463 for the two quotes.

didly expressed by Proclus by the term "awakening," as if from sleep. For just as sensible things which we meet externally recollect what we had known beforehand, similarly sensible mathematical things , if they are recognized, therefore, elicit intellectual things which are previously present within, so that things now in actuality shine forth in the soul which were hidden in it before, as if under a veil of potentiality. How then, did it break in? I reply that the *ideas or formal causes* [E.S. emphasis] of the harmonies, in accordance with our earlier discussion of them, are completely innate in those who possess this power of recognition but they are not after all taken within them by contemplation, but rather depend on a natural instinct, and are innate in them, as the number, (something intellectual) of the leaves in the flower and of the segments in a fruit are innate in the *forms* [E.S. emphasis] of plants.[72]

72. Kepler, **The Harmony of the World**, translated by E.J. Aiton, A.M. Duncan, and J.V. Field, (Philadelphia: American Philosophical

I find it striking that nowadays formative causation is not considered, perhaps because we tend to reject immaterial causes in physics, and it isn't considered necessary to ask how such great minds came to the idea, even by the scholars who translate their works. It might qualify as what Plato, Leibniz, and LaRouche called "innate ideas."

Although Leibniz used the term "substantial form" to be the immaterial entity which governs vis viva, live force, he eschewed its use to account for morphogenesis. The latter he treated as determined at the Creation by "Preformation." This may have been related to his idea that the monad has a program and is not directly influenced by its environment. [73]

LaRouche has written that the mind is distinct from the brain in the sense that is not merely an epiphenomenon of the brain, so that cognition is an independent physical principle in the universe; the three domains of the abiotic, the living and cognition being multiply connected. In his discussion of Gurwitsch's biological field, which Gurwitsch said regulated morphogenesis, LaRouche characterized its action as "not a discrete memory, simply genetic-mechanical, but rather some developmental impulse within the living process which follows a least-action pathway in respect to its relationship to its own previous development and its setting. This, again, is precisely what we find in physical economy."[74] He seems to be describing an imbedded intention in the development of the embryo.

I believe we may be dealing with the generally overlooked relation of mind, in whatever its particular concrete form, and matter. LaRouche emphasized: "The issue of the way in which living processes serve as the medium in which the development of cognition has occurred, is the key challenge for all the fundamental issues of modern scientific knowledge."[75]

Society, 1997). The quote is from pages 307-308 of Book IV.
73. This article has a good discussion of the role of current biological thinking in Leibniz's monadology. Leibniz referred often to microscopic biological observations in support. Salvatore Russo, "The Influence of the Theory of Preformation on Leibniz's Metaphysics, 1931" (The Open Court).
74. Lyndon LaRouche's Remarks on Gurwitsch's method in **21st Century Science and Technology**, page 57, Fall 1998.
75. Lyndon LaRouche, "On the Subject of Education,"